D1084125

CREATIVE
OUTDOOR
PLAY
AREAS

PEGGY L. MILLER

Michigan Department of Education

CREATIVE
OUTDOOR
PLAY
AREAS

Prentice-Hall, Inc., Englewood Cliffs, New Jersey

252515

© 1972 by Prentice-Hall, Inc., Englewood Cliffs, New Jersey

All rights reserved. No part of this book may be reproduced in any form or by any means without permission in writing from the publisher.

ISBN: 0-13-190595-3

Library of Congress Catalog Card Number: 73-38798

Printed in the United States of America

10 9 8 7 6 5 4 3 2 1

JV
424
m47

PRENTICE-HALL INTERNATIONAL, INC., *London*
PRENTICE-HALL OF AUSTRALIA, PTY. LTD., *Sydney*
PRENTICE-HALL OF CANADA, LTD., *Toronto*
PRENTICE-HALL OF INDIA PRIVATE LIMITED, *New Delhi*
PRENTICE-HALL OF JAPAN, INC., *Tokyo*

This book is dedicated to my father, Orlo W. Miller,
whose life was devoted to the education of children and youth.
He strove to help others achieve physical, mental, and spiritual
health and fitness. He had a special interest in wholesome creative
outdoor play not only for his own children but for youngsters
everywhere. He was the inspiration for the writing of this book.

Contents

3

**General Guidelines
for Developing
Creative Outdoor
Play Areas, 17**

4

**Specific Guidelines
for Developing
Creative Outdoor
Play Areas, 25**

5

**Natural
Topographical
Features, 31**

6

**Creative
Play
Equipment, 37**

7

**Examples of
Comprehensive
Play Areas, 63**

Foreword

THE MESSAGE IN THIS BOOK IS TIMELY. In a day of complexity, fraught with tensions and uncertainties, much more time and effort must be devoted to providing an environment conducive to the normal growth of children. The concentration of a large portion of the population in cities, the shrinking open spaces, and sedentary living have imposed serious restrictions on "just being a child" for great numbers of the young. Our society is largely adult-centered, and unlike their forebears, today's children lack many of the advantages offered by a more simple form of living, where open spaces and natural beauty abound.

The picture is not as dark as it may seem, however, for much more is known about growth and learning than is practiced—there is an increasing concern about improving the quality of living for all our people, and through good planning there can be places where children may have a "childhood," where play can be a natural and integral part of the learning process. Furthermore, many educators, parents, and leaders of community agencies are aware that the talents of *all* children, wherever they may live, and regardless of socio-economic status or color of skin, can be developed. There are bright spots here and there where education becomes real and meaningful to each individual child through learning experiences in life situations. Outdoor education is one of the modern emphases in education which helps extend the curriculum beyond the classroom into the outdoors where learning is vital and *fun*.

For many children, the opportunity for creative play under open skies may be their first exposure to the outdoors—where they perceive of themselves as a part of the living universe, and where they may become "whole beings."

The author of this book is uniquely qualified to capture the potentials of joining the play instinct of children with outdoor settings, which free the physical, mental, and spiritual talents for creative endeavors. Her own talents, which have found expression in sports skills, creative crafts, music, writing, and leadership, have provided a rich background for innovations in many aspects of education, including play. A broad background of experiences in several levels of education, elementary, secondary, and college, combined with advanced graduate study in curriculum, communications, and outdoor education, have enabled her to place creative play in proper perspective in the educative process and to perceive the kind of planning, resources, and leadership necessary to provide better educational opportunities for this generation of children. Creative outdoor play areas can, in the midst of today's complex world, provide some good places for today's children who will be tomorrow's citizens.

Julian W. Smith
College of Education
Michigan State University

Preface

THIS BOOK HAS BEEN WRITTEN for a variety of readers, including professional educators, architects, real estate developers, city planners, parents, park and recreation area designers, and students of physical education. It is hoped that all those who are concerned about providing wholesome creative outdoor play areas for children and youth may gain some ideas here.

This book is especially directed towards improving the play areas provided on *school sites* where children probably spend more time in play activities than anywhere else. The school play area, undoubtedly the most common kind of outdoor play area, is found in varying degrees of quality and sophistication wherever there is a school building. The school play area is a place where planned and unplanned learning opportunities are provided under the auspices of the school. Therefore play on the school playground is part of the school curriculum. Thus it deserves close attention by educators who are directly responsible for all the learning opportunities provided by the school. It is unfortunate that while school buildings, educational policies, teaching methods, and learning materials have been changing rapidly during recent years, school play areas have remained almost the same over the past several decades. Educators and school architects who are involved in the planning, development, and operation of school play areas may find the ideas presented herein to be useful.

The book also presents possibilities for the improvement and development of *municipal parks,* whether they be large or small, in great cities or small towns. Special attention is given to what are being termed *mini parks* or vest pocket parks in urban areas—inner city locations as well as other congested metropolitan settings. The federal government has provided grants to municipalities to build these tiny parks as part of the federal Open Space Land Program administered by the Department of Housing and Urban Development. Under the federal regulations, a city must match the amount of the federal grant with local funds. Even in inner cities there are vacant lots and little pieces of unused land. They are often nothing more than depositories for junk and trash. Through careful planning and a minimal amount of money, much of this wasted urban land can be restored and used constructively—for children's learning.

The yards of *private homes* have potential for becoming creative play areas. A child's home environment has a major effect upon his growth and development, especially during the preschool and early elementary school years. Parents can plan, design, and provide home play areas that are more conducive to the healthy growth of their children.

Shopping centers which provide play areas where children may stay while their parents shop have potential for becoming creative outdoor play areas. In addition, this book discusses application of the concept of creative outdoor play areas in large *real estate developments,* including *town house* and *apartment complexes.*

It is believed that the ideas presented here are practical and feasible for the improvement and development of play areas in *state* and *county recreation areas,* and in *roadside parks,* including *expressway cases.* There are applications to private *nursery schools, churches, children's hospitals, summer camps,* and *outdoor drive-in theaters,* all which often provide outdoor play areas for youngsters.

Acknowledgments

Special recognition and appreciation are given to the following: *Journal of Outdoor Education* for the right to quote an article by H. Clifton Hutchins; George Kochaniec of the *Macomb Daily News* for permission to reproduce the photograph found on page 88; Fran Evert, Photographer (Farmington, Michigan) for permission to use the photographs taken at the Bloomfield Hills Public Schools found on pages 68, 73, 76, 78, and 81; and Kenneth Kumasawa for permission to reproduce the photographs found on pages xviii, 10, 16, 62, 98, 106, and 112.

The author is indebted to the many people who have written about and built good play areas in various locales of the country.

Grateful acknowledgement is also extended to Wendy Miller Severson, the author's sister, for the illustrations which appear in this publication.

A debt of gratitude is due to the author's parents, Dorothy L. Miller and the late Orlo W. Miller, who provided an outstanding educative home in which to grow up. Many of their ideas are perpetuated herein.

Special appreciation is expressed to the author's former professors at the University of Wisconsin and Michigan State University who helped her gain a broad understanding of how youngsters grow and learn, particularly to Dr. Julian W. Smith, recognized for his pioneer work in outdoor education.

P. L. M.

CREATIVE
OUTDOOR
PLAY
AREAS

1

Play
and
Children's Learning

LEARNING IS THE RESULT of experiences which occur in a number of environments—the home, the school, the neighborhood, and the church, among others. In general, the more widespread and varied these experiences are, the broader the education will be.

Experiences facilitate the growth of individuals while deprivation of experiences limits it. When experiential deprivation of experiences occurs in the formative years of infancy and childhood, it becomes extremely difficult for persons to reach their full physical, social, intellectual, and emotional potentials.

In a certain sense all individuals are products of their environments. Thus it is important to provide rich environments in which individuals may live, in order to realize the best possible "products."

The outdoors is always an educative environment, sometimes positive, sometimes negative. For most children and youth, the outdoors can be one of the most important environmental influences upon their lives. Greater attention and consideration should be given to the kinds and quality of learning experiences which the outdoors can provide.

Outdoor play areas are outdoor classrooms. They can provide rich opportunities for youngsters to gain educative experiences through play, which is a major means of learning for children. Unfortunately, some play areas provide children with a great many negative learning experiences. The majority of outdoor play areas are places of tradition, basically unchanged in design since the late 1800s and early 1900s when playgrounds were first built in this country. They are today as they were then—equipment of steel or iron bars, surfaces of concrete or asphalt, with steel fencing around everything. These play areas have been built to "keep kids off the streets," yet the streets are often much more attractive to youngsters than these sterile, cold, drab, and unimaginative playgrounds. The deficiencies of these typical, traditional play areas, in terms of their potential for providing desirable learning experiences, are numerous.

It is imperative that outdoor play areas, so influential upon youngsters' lives, be studied and improved. The opportunities for learning which they provide through a variety of experiences must be enhanced so that outdoor play areas will contribute positively to the education of boys and girls. That is the purpose of this book.

Universality of Play

Many things once thought to be changeless are being altered. But in a world of constant change play still follows age-old patterns, for children's play, through many centuries, has maintained essentially the same features. This is true for the play of children who live in vastly different cultures—it has the same basic characteristics, and takes the same form. The play of the American Indian children of the nineteenth century did not differ appreciably from the play of eighteenth-century English children. The play of eighteenth-century Chinese children was not really different from the play of today's Mexican children. Likewise, there is no appreciable distinction between the basic play patterns of the American millionaire's three-year-old and those of the poor man's three-year-old. Generally speaking, all children play the same way.

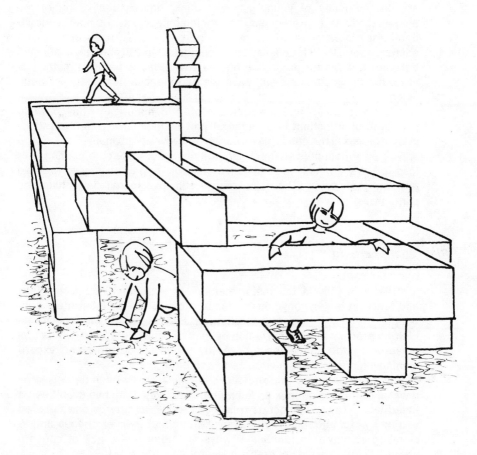

The Play Instinct

Play is a basic need of childhood. There is a play instinct in each child, a need to play and move in particular patterns and to carry out certain activities which will help bring about the maturation process. This pertains not only to the child's physical growth, but also to his social and mental development. Large muscle movements, so characteristic of childhood play, are a basic instinct in youngsters.

This need for play which brings about desirable growth and development for adulthood is also evidenced by animals. Those who have observed the young of the various species of the animal kingdom have noted the play patterns in which all young animals engage. These patterns include large body movements and imitations of the mother's movements. Running, jumping, dodging, tumbling, and rolling activities are characteristic of young animals' play. Play by the young of the animal world is a prerequisite for their achievement of mature adulthood. Play is essential to the maturation process. Through play, young animals learn the responses, the techniques, the procedures, and the behavior needed for protection and survival. Play is nature's method of assuring that youngsters will have the experiences necessary for adult living.

A baby, a child, and a youth all "play to maturity." They *have* to play. The play instinct is an integral part of their growth and development process. They must play in order to grow up normally.

The play instinct is so ingrained in individuals that some adults never lose it. Many adults love to play like children long after they've reached physical maturation. These individuals still love to roll down hills and climb trees!

Play and Learning

Children's play is the major medium of learning for children. Play and learning are synonymous terms and constitute an integrated, continuous process in the lives of children. Play is the initial stage in the lifelong process of learning which every individual experiences. It is life-research by the child—the process by which he explores and experiments with himself, his environment, and other people.

Play to some adults, unfortunately, has historically been perceived as a waste or misuse of time, a "killing time" activity. Play has even been a hated word. This is almost as true today as it was fifty or one hundred and fifty years ago. Many adults currently reflect their erroneous understanding of play in a number of ways, including their lack of concern about and attention to children's play areas.

What children learn in the poorly planned and sterile play areas commonly found today, what they learn from playing in the streets of urban areas, what they learn from repetitive seesawing, sliding, and swinging, is greatly inferior to what they learn in creative play areas planned by people who understand the needs, interests, and potentials of children and know that play is significant learning.

Play fosters and maximizes children's growth and development. It is necessary for the maturation of children. Play is a great natural urge of children from infancy to adulthood through which they gain significant learnings in the cognitive, affective, and psychomotor domains. Play for children *is* simultaneously a cognitive, psychomotor, and affective experience. Without these learnings which form a foundation for later and more complex neurological, social, and psychological learnings, some children will never grow and develop properly. Recent studies by medical and educational researchers in the area of learning disabilities dramatically confirm these observations. To put it another way, play and the learnings which accrue through play are prerequisites for later learnings which the individual must gain to achieve full maturation.

Children need motor, verbal, social, visual, and other kinds of stimulation to develop fully and to attain their potential. Numerous studies of disadvantaged inner city and rural children show that they are "disadvantaged" because they lack experiences which provide these kinds of stimulation. If these children are to have a fair chance in life, competing with their "advantaged" contemporaries, they must be provided opportunities to gain the stimulating experiences so vital to their optimal growth and development. Through wisely planned and maintained play-learning areas, disadvantaged youngsters can achieve many of these experiences.

We must more fully appreciate the value of the play of a child ". . . from which he gains in knowledge through direct sensory experience, from which he enriches his spirit with the security of companionship and the discovery of beauty in his surroundings, and from which he grows in stature and maturity by making demands on his vital organs, musculature and coordination." [1]

The Importance of Play in Overall Development

Play is essential to the development of (1) basic motor skills including perceptual-motor development, and physical fitness and growth; (2) mental skills; (3) social skills; and (4) emotional maturity.

Basic motor skills. Play contributes to the physical growth, motor development, physiological functioning, and physical fitness of youngsters.

---

[1] H. Clifton Hutchins, "Learning About Leisure in Relation to the Environment," *Journal of Outdoor Education*, Fall, 1970, p. 17.

Through play they instinctively, and on a rather regular basis, practice the basic motor skills of jumping, running, hopping, walking, throwing, and leaping in varied forms and combinations.

Through sensory motor activity, which according to Piaget and others is the primary mode of learning in young children, youngsters develop skills in their perception of body positions and movement in space, and awareness of their environment and of themselves distinct from their surroundings. To accomplish these activities, both gross motor and fine manipulative movements are necessary. Coordination, agility, balance, strength, and endurance are all acquired through swinging, climbing, walking balance beams, and other activities.

The acquisition of these basic motor skills or movement patterns not only allows the child to function adequately in the present, but has significant implications for his future living:

1. These movement patterns are the basis for his future recreational pursuits.

2. These movement patterns are the basis for his future mental activity. Human development is characterized by an orderly progression of changes in physical development and body structure from infancy through adolescence. A broad base of fundamental motor skills (a variety of motor experiences) is necessary for the sequential and systematic mental growth and development of the individual, according to Piaget. Some people term this relationship "perceptual-motor development," and refer to a failure to achieve full perceptual-motor development as "learning disability." Many youngsters exhibiting learning problems in fact have inadequately developed perceptual-motor skills.

To put it another way, there are stages in development which must be learned and practiced in the correct order if maturation is to be achieved. The child moves through certain developmental levels or stages on his way to becoming an adult. Motor development is a prerequisite for mental development. There is a considerable amount of research which indicates a positive correlation between motor development and mental abilities and performance.

The late Jay B. Nash, one of the great proponents of the importance of motor skills in the growth of individuals, often pointed out that these skills, particularly those involving the hands, preceded the development of the mind in the history of the race. He referred to this process as "muscling in on the mind."

Mental development.   Play provides children with opportunities to engage in problem solving, particularly if play occurs in creative settings. Problem-solving skills are among the most important skills to be learned for living in today's rapidly changing world.

Through play youngsters learn communication skills, especially oral language development. They learn the meaning of words and other symbols. They learn how words are put together to form phrases and sentences.

Concepts such as shape, number, force, texture, and frequency are developed through play. Children learn to classify, find order, distinguish between natural and unnatural, label, discover differences, and match.

Play provides children with a backlog of experiences and knowledge with which they can make wise choices and decisions in the present and in the future. Play is an integral part of the educative process, the major purpose of which, according to the Educational Policies Commission, is to help the individual think and make rational choices.[2]

Social development. Children learn socialization skills through play. They grow away from the egoism which characterizes the infant and young child, and become more other-centered.

In children's play they emulate older youngsters' and adults' ways of doing things and their relationships with others. They learn the roles of youth and adulthood. They learn the values of their peers, their elders, and of society as a whole. They prepare, through play, to assume the tasks, activities, and the desirable human relationships of daily living as mature persons. They learn leadership and "followership" skills and roles.

Through play children learn about, and grow to understand, other people. They learn attitudes. They learn about cooperation, the rights of self in relation to the rights of others, compromise, teamwork, sharing, conflict resolution, and group decision making. The play skills of children are often the basis for youngsters' social relations.

Children and youth must satisfy what Jay B. Nash called the "activity urge." [3] Through activities in creative outdoor play areas they can satisfy this urge in constructive, socially acceptable, and beneficial ways. If opportunities are not provided for constructive social development, antisocial behavior will be practiced and learned as a means by which to satisfy this "activity urge."

In this era of misunderstanding and hatred between people of differing races, nationalities, religions, and socio-economic backgrounds, the play of little children can erase all differences. They do not perceive such artificial boundaries between themselves and others. Children's play is a great equalizer of men. Children of diverse backgrounds can, through play, build bridges between men; they can establish a new social order in a world of social chaos.

Emotional development. Through play activities children grow and develop in understanding and knowledge of themselves as individuals.

[2] Educational Policies Commission, *The Central Purpose of American Education* (Washington, D.C.: National Education Association, 1961).
[3] Jay B. Nash, *Philosophy of Recreation and Leisure* (Dubuque, Iowa: William C Brown Company, Publishers, 1960), pp. 83–84.

Play builds a concept of self and a sense of body image. Self-esteem is affected by play. The child develops a deeper awareness of himself in his physical world and in relation to others. Play helps establish for the child the concept of "who am I."

The child learns self-confidence, self-reliance, and independence, especially if he is provided opportunities to engage in "risk play." He learns what he can and can't do, his abilities and his limitations. The child must take risks in order to achieve the more difficult—that step just beyond his present experience, ability, and grasp—in order to learn and grow.

The child learns self-expression and self-discipline as he plays. He expresses his inner feelings through play. It is an outlet for his energy, and sometimes for his anger and frustration. It is far more constructive for the child to express these emotions through climbing, running, and swinging, than to break lamps, hit siblings, or physically hurt himself. In play the child plays out or acts out happy and unhappy situations which he has confronted or experienced. Play can thus contribute to good mental health.

Through play children build their own individual value systems. Through wholesome play activities, children gain emotional fitness. Play contributes to the quality of children's inner space—their minds and their hearts.

Play and Creativity

Play provides children with ways to express their creative urges, opportunities to perceive objects, and chances to put things together in new ways; to reorganize, to give a different use to something; to achieve a new relationship with another; and to interpret in an alternate way. Play can provide the individual with opportunities for imaginative acting and thinking, and for fantasy which is important to emotional development. Play providing creative expression helps the individual to define and understand himself.

All children need to express creativity, which is inherent in every human being. Everyone is endowed with latent talents, some of which can find early expression through play. All too often, the creativity of children is unwittingly suppressed in the adult-centered world, even in the schools. The opportunity for free play may well be a key to unlock the store of creative talents allotted to each human being.

Creation is a human need. If youngsters don't have ways in which to be creative, if outlets for the creative instinct are not provided, their development and growth are severely limited. Some believe that when creativity is thwarted, delinquent behavior is encouraged; in this view, creativity and delinquency or unsocial activity are on two opposite ends of a behavior continuum.

Well-planned play areas with their opportunities for creative expression are integral and inseparable parts of a rich learning environment. These kinds of outdoor settings, with their low levels of threatening activity, are necessary for creative expression. An environment which provides many creative play opportunities will allow the child to have some "success experiences." These will help him develop a good self-concept and perceive that he is worthy of respect.

2

The Importance of Outdoor Play

Vanishing Play Spaces

OUTDOOR PLAY IS GREATLY RESTRICTED in American culture today. Outdoor space is vanishing rapidly. Over 75 percent of Americans live in urban areas. Little space in these urban areas has been reserved for grass and trees, and places where youngsters have enough room to play. Conditions today are much different from the quite recent past when the majority of Americans lived in rural areas.

In the past there was abundant space available for the play of children and youth. The play of yesteryear was chiefly characterized by running games. In today's urban areas very little space is available where much running can occur. Many city schools are built on pitifully small pieces of land, and the little free space available for children's play is black-topped and restrictive. City parks are all too frequently inadequate in terms of size, and too distant from the homes of many youngsters to be easily accessible. Gone also are the vacant lots, large and small, where many of today's adults once ran, jumped, climbed, and leaped. Outdoor space adequate in terms of size, and accessible in terms of location, is a vanishing commodity in America today and virtually unknown to the millions of children and youths who live cramped together, in and around our cities. Yet youngsters, and all people, need space for living productively.

Today's Sedentary Habits

American adults are not only failing to provide adequate outdoor space in which children may play, but the majority of adults are setting poor examples for children in terms of their own life activity or life style. Most adults lead very sedentary lives; many of them consciously, as well as unconsciously, urge youngsters to lead similar lives. These parents, teachers, and others who act as "models" for young people in fact do them a disfavor.

These adult "models," these "significant others" in youngsters' lives, spend most of their time sitting, standing, resting, watching television, riding in automobiles, eating, and going to the movies. Many of these adults would not be able to protect or save themselves, if necessary, by running or climbing in situations of stress, danger, or catastrophe. When weather conditions are even slightly adverse, most adults do not venture outdoors (except to walk to their cars); and many of them prohibit their children or students from playing outdoors, even when the youngsters desire to do so. Thus adults consciously and unconsciously set life patterns for children.

Rather than helping young people to learn to live in harmony with the outdoors during the variety of seasons, to enjoy playing in the snow as well as in the summer sunshine, most adults teach children that the outdoors is a place to be used and enjoyed only at certain times of the year, in certain weather conditions, at certain times of the day. Many youngsters, therefore, are deprived of the joys of knowing and playing in the outdoors under all conditions. American children spend too much time sitting and viewing in indoor settings. The number of hours per day during which the average American youngster watches television, gaining only vicarious experience, is astounding and shameful. Such sedentary habits deprive young people of the movement patterns, socialization, and other skills they need in order to achieve maximum, high-quality growth and development.

Ignorance of Outdoor Skills

Those who neither play nor live outdoors on a regular basis lack the skills and knowledge to enjoy and use it well on the rare occasions that they do venture outdoors. The outdoor "illiteracy" of the majority of our nation's adults is obvious. On those infrequent occasions when the outdoor illiterates decide to engage in some weekend fishing, take a two-week camping trip, or even visit a park for a cookout, their lack of outdoor knowledge and skills is both amusing and pitiful, and the ventures often result in unhappy experiences. Only through instruction and actual experience outdoors in a variety of settings and over an extended period of time do people gain knowledge and skills for worthwhile and satisfying outdoor living and outdoor experiences. Children who have been provided the rich experiences which result from playing in the outdoors throughout their childhoods will have the skills, understanding, and appreciation as adults to gain happy and worthwhile outdoor experiences. They will have developed a repertoire of outdoor activities, skills, and interests from which to draw.

"Worthy Use of Leisure"

Americans suffer from leisure misuse and abuse. This is ironic when one considers the fact that Americans have more free time than any other people of the world. The problem lies with the lack of skills which adults possess to make wise use of the hours they do not spend working, eating, and sleeping. It is believed that for the most part, leisure time patterns are established early in life; that skills which adults use in their free time are learned in childhood. Educators recognized this years ago when they included "worthy use of leisure time" as a prime goal of American education in the "Seven Cardinal Principles of Education." Adults who do engage in worthwhile leisure activities, upon analysis of their particular skills and interests, almost always trace them back to beginnings in childhood days. Leisure skills for the outdoors, or the indoors, are predominantly learned during childhood. Thus it is important that children and youth are provided creative outdoor play areas so that they may learn there outdoor skills and interests which will carry over into the leisure hours of their adult years.

Inherent Richness of Natural Environments

Children and youth in the natural outdoor environment are exposed to a wealth of play and learning opportunities. They don't need devices; they make their own play equipment from the many natural resources at hand. But all the natural things—trees, streams, boulders, and grassy hillsides—provided by nature are disappearing. Gone are many of nature's provisions for youngsters' play. The object of the creative outdoor play area is, in part, to highlight or feature some of the resources of the natural rural outdoors in a man-made environment. Special attention must be given to the design of urban play areas to make up for the loss of trees to climb, streams in which to cool hot dusty feet, and stone walls upon which to walk and balance.

There is a direct relationship between knowing the outdoors and appreciating it. There is a direct relationship between appreciating the outdoors and protecting it and improving its quality. Youngsters who grow up playing in the outdoors in a variety of outdoor settings and learning about it will be children and eventually adults who will seek to preserve and improve the outdoors for themselves and others. These children and adults will be concerned about pollution, overpopulation, extinction of animal and plant species, and other problems.

Moreover, youngsters need beneficial conditions, a healthful environment in which to play. Children need pollution-free air; they need clean water, adequate space, quiet areas, and places free from nails and trash. In thinking about creative outdoor play, the present national and world-wide concern about the quality of the outdoors must be considered carefully.

Through extended opportunities for good outdoor play, youngsters will come to establish a oneness with nature. They will realize their role in the ecology spectrum.

Quality of Life

Discussed in the preceding section is quality of life, or quality of living. Greater attention must be given to the quality of every single day's living. Greater attention must be given to the experiences which children are daily provided, purposely and unintentionally. Living patterns are established early in life. Providing children and youth with various experiences of living and learning in wholesome outdoor settings will have positive effects upon their patterns of living. The outdoors is and can continue to be a rich environment for learning and living for people of all ages.

3

General Guidelines for Developing Creative Outdoor Play Areas

PLANNING FOR THE DEVELOPMENT of creative outdoor play areas ought to be based upon some general guidelines. To ignore these guidelines in the development of play areas would be to build a house without a foundation.

Identifying and Meeting
Children's Needs and Interests

Settings, activities, and opportunities promoting learning should be the foremost consideration in developing creative outdoor play areas. They should be built upon children's needs, not adults' needs. They should be child-centered, not equipment-centered. After the youngsters' needs are identified, attention should be given to other aspects of developing a creative outdoor play area, including the selection of natural topographical features and the design of equipment.

Often, unfortunately, the emphasis in developing play areas is unduly placed upon the site, and not upon the children and youth who will use the area. The area itself is often viewed as an end in itself, while it should be regarded only as a means to the real end—the well-being of children and youth.

Children's interests as well as their needs should be provided for and reflected in creative outdoor play areas. Unless children's interests are ascertained and provided for, children will not be motivated to engage in activity.

By talking with children and observing their free and spontaneous play activities in the outdoors and elsewhere, adults can gain clues and direct information about youngsters' interests. Adults need help in discovering what young people consider important. Thus the inspiration and direction for the development of creative outdoor play areas can and should be gained primarily from children themselves (and perhaps, too, from adults' memories of what they loved best to play with when they were young).

What things do children love? Here are some of them.

Children love to move! They love to swing, balance, climb, jump, leap, hop, throw, skip, and most of all, run! Children today especially need room for running.

Children love adventure, thrills, challenge! Children love to be "stretched" physically, mentally, and emotionally; they like to be challenged in skills. They like to take small risks and prove themselves successful in meeting them. They love to jump the width of a stream, climb to the top of a tree, balance on a tilted log, and crawl to the top of a rockpile.

Children love to build! They love to construct rafts, bridges, trains, boats, cars, houses, tents, tunnels, and, most of all, forts. Children make forts out of culverts, hollow trees, tables and other furniture overspread with blankets, bushes with low arching branches, crates, big cardboard boxes, barrels, and ravines covered with boards. They love to feel protected, snug, and isolated in their forts. They love to build their own play things, and they learn while building them. They express their creativity by choosing and utilizing ordinary materials found in their surroundings in new ways.

Children love to pretend! They imitate actual experiences they'd like to have. They love to imitate daddy at work, mother cooking dinner, sister getting ready for a dance, brother going deer hunting. They pretend to drive cars, fly airplanes, catch fish, and keep house, just like their elders. They pretend to be horses, monkeys, pigs, and dragons. They imitate cowboys, football players, and astronauts. They pretend to be supermen, magicians, princesses, goblins, witches, and fairy godmothers.

Children love to play in the soil! Children love to dig, rake, hoe, and carry dirt in pails and wheelbarrows. They love to water their little "gardens." They love to dig for worms. They love to make piles of dirt, snow, sand, and leaves, and then jump in them. They love to bury and dig for "hidden treasure." Someone has said that it's just as important for children to have their hands in soil as it is for them to have vitamins.

Children love to hide! They love the delicious feeling of being sought for and the anticipation of being found behind a tree, in a ditch, under bushes, in a barrel—anywhere which provides a temporary safety from the seeking eyes of others!

Children love to throw! They love to throw mud balls, snow balls, rocks, pebbles, shells, sticks, cans, or anything else on hand, whether the target is inanimate or moving, human or animal!

Children love to play with and in water!   They love lawn hoses and sprinklers, faucets, ponds, mud puddles, streams, lakes, swimming pools, rivers, bogs, springs, watering troughs, and marshes. They love boats, rafts, piers, and docks. They love to fish (even without real hooks and bait), net minnows, wade, sail toy boats, swim, and dangle their bare feet in cool water.

Children love to balance!   They love to balance on the tops of fences, walk on railroad tracks, teeter on fallen logs, and skip along the tops of stone and brick walls.

If play areas do not meet children's interests, youngsters will go elsewhere to seek excitement and challenge, and often find it in delinquent and antisocial activities.

Designing for Children

Creative outdoor play areas should be planned for the use of many kinds of participants. The following specific groups of youngsters should be provided for:

Preschool children.   Creative outdoor play areas should be provided for all preschool children, including toddlers. These youngsters should be provided new experiences in the outdoors away from the familiar indoor environments of the home, and other places where they spend time. The preschool participants should include disadvantaged as well as advantaged children. The cumulative motor development which results from creative play is essential for this age group.

Elementary school children.   Outdoor play areas traditionally have been designed primarily for this age group. But the particular needs and interests of the early elementary grades, the later elementary grades, and disadvantaged children, especially those participating in programs such as Follow Through and ESEA Title I, should be better reflected in creative outdoor play areas. Again, certain perceptual-motor development outcomes which are gained through wholesome play are absolutely essential for the maturation process of these children.

Secondary school youth.   This population should be served by creative outdoor play areas in two major ways. First, play areas should be designed to meet their needs for, and interests in, play, as much as needs are met for younger children. Youth is pushed into growing up too quickly, and deprived of some of the joys of being young. Youth should be encouraged to engage more in wholesome play activities, instead of being influenced to imitate adults in sophisticated and oftentimes unhealthful pursuits. Youth ought to be provided with opportunities to find thrills and adventure through healthful play, instead of being left to find thrills and adventure through delinquent behavior, which they will do if there are no alternatives. Perhaps Outward Bound and similar programs are multiplying because they are successfully supplying challenging and thrilling play opportunities for older youth.

Second, this age group should be involved in the actual development of creative outdoor play areas for younger children and themselves. They should take part in area planning, construction of equipment, landscaping, and maintenance. All of these activities can be meaningful learning experiences provided for in the school curriculum in the areas of art, home economics, industrial arts, science, physical education, health education, and others.

Handicapped youngsters.   The needs and interests of crippled and otherwise physically handicapped, mentally retarded, emotionally disturbed, blind, deaf and hard of hearing, and multihandicapped children should be met by creative outdoor play areas. Special features can be included for these youngsters, especially for the blind and crippled. While the play areas should allow for the implementation of specific individual "learning prescriptions," opportunities ought to be provided for handicapped children to engage in self-directed play activities, because so many aspects of their lives are directed by others for them. Creative outdoor play areas offer many experiences for these young people which will enrich their lives and increase their learning and facilitate their adjustment.

Students who are behavior problems. By providing these students with opportunities for wholesome play and purposeful outdoor work experiences as part of their school program, their involvement in creative outdoor play areas can prove to be highly successful.

Using Basic Learning Principles Effectively

Knowledge about the learning patterns of youngsters should be reviewed and then reflected in creative outdoor play areas, whenever they are built or rebuilt. The following learning principles have implications:

1. There is a natural desire in every individual to learn. Build upon the natural motivation and interest of youngsters.
2. Through *doing,* significant learning is gained. Individuals learn by *active* participation.
3. Through opportunities to perceive with all the senses—touching, tasting, hearing, smelling, and seeing—significant learning is gained.
4. When the individual deals with *concretes,* instead of abstracts, significant learning is gained.
5. When threat to oneself is low, learning is aided. A distinction should be made between "challenge" and "threat."
6. When the "whole" person is involved in an experience, learning is more lasting and pervasive.
7. Learning "in context" is more significant than learning "in isolation."
8. All learners are unique. They differ in learning ability, rate, and style. Individual differences must be accepted and allowances made for them.
9. Each learner may facilitate the learning of another. Children learn from each other.

Adaptability of Play Areas

Since play areas should be developed on the basis of children's needs and interests, and since children's needs and interests are continually changing, play areas themselves should be subject to change. Play areas should be versatile, adaptable, and flexible. Equipment should be moveable. Growing, developing, and changing children need changing play areas.

Involving Children in
Planning and Development

Children and youth should play an active and responsible role in designing, constructing, interpreting, and maintaining creative outdoor play areas. In so doing, they are more likely to use, protect, and care for them. Creative outdoor play areas should be youngsters' territories, not adults'. Youngsters should interpret for themselves, through opportunities for individual choices, how the space, topography, and equipment will be used. Opportunities should exist for some structured, adult-directed learning activities, but individual and group child-directed spontaneous free play should predominate.

4

Specific Guidelines for Developing Creative Outdoor Play Areas

A NUMBER OF SPECIFIC GUIDELINES must be given consideration in the development of creative outdoor play areas. For a high-quality play area, it is imperative that these guidelines be heeded.

Integration of Land Areas

Give attention to the land around and adjacent to the creative outdoor play area, and, whenever possible, integrate the two. This is especially important when the play area is part of a large park, recreation area, school site, or school outdoor education laboratory.

Natural Features of the Site

Utilize natural features within and adjacent to the play area. The natural qualities of the site should be preserved. The topography should be accentuated, not destroyed. Too often the land is cleared by bulldozer for the placement of manufactured steel equipment. But mounds, hills, trees, plants, streams, boulders, and other natural features should be integral parts of the play area.

Natural Space

Many adults fail to appreciate natural space. They are disposed to look upon space altered by man as the only legitimate place for play. This is particularly true in regard to school play areas. In actuality, however, children value and are motivated by natural space, and engage spontaneously in a variety of play activities. Those who value natural space realize that the more manufactured things are put in natural areas, the more restricted the utilization of the natural space becomes. Some play areas could well be composed entirely of natural things; others should be balanced wisely between natural and man-made things.

26

Attractiveness

Make the creative outdoor play area aesthetically pleasing. It should be attractive in terms of color, shape, and texture. Inner city play areas should be green spots and places of beauty in contrast to the surrounding environment. Individual pieces of play equipment should be harmoniously related to other equipment, as well as blended with the natural features of the area.

Materials for Equipment

Use inexpensive and easily accessible materials for play equipment, especially natural materials such as logs, flagstones, tree stumps, and railroad ties, as well as any other unsophisticated objects children tend to choose for play in natural environments. Too often equipment for play areas is adult oriented; it is made to attract adult buyers, not child users. Furthermore, children and youth should be allowed and encouraged to bring their own equipment and tools to the play area, including rope, wire, canvas, poles, tires, and boxes.

Community Resources and Involvement

Assess existing community resources. Gather information on the number of public and private play areas present in the community, including schools. Find out location, sizes, kinds of equipment provided, and age group served by each. Identify and contact service clubs and individuals who might be willing to donate services and resources to the planning and development of creative outdoor play areas. Locate manufacturers or businessmen who might be willing to give or sell supplies, services, and equipment at wholesale or reduced prices.

Seek and utilize the cooperation and help of parents, service club members, government representatives, educators, and other community people in planning for and developing play areas. Elementary, junior, and senior high school youngsters should be involved in varying degrees in the planning, building, and maintenance of these areas.

Safety

Give consideration to the safety of youngsters. Planning for safety, including traffic control and the maintenance of equipment, should be a continuous process. The equipment should be the kind requiring little or no adult supervision. Careful location of equipment is important. The play area should be developed so that when the inevitable tumbles and collisions occur, children's bruises and hurts will be minor. Unfortunately, safety has not been an important consideration in the design of many play areas, particularly those traditional ones composed largely of asphalt surfaces with steel or iron equipment, such as slides, swings, teeter-totters, merry-go-rounds, and giant strides. Play areas such as these almost guarantee serious accidents. In a school district known to the author, where 42 accidents occurred in a four-month period, one-half happened on school playgrounds, all of the traditional kind.

Specific safety considerations should include the following: height of equipment; stability of equipment; ease of supervision of play area; kinds of surfaces, particularly those beneath equipment; hand- or footholds and gripping surfaces on equipment; weather factors, including shade, rain, sun, and wind; and the degree to which youngsters of varying age groups are mixed in the play area. One important thing to remember when considering safety is that most youngsters will do only what they feel reasonably comfortable doing; they usually will not push themselves beyond levels at which they are skilled and feel fairly secure.

Individual and Group Use

Provide for maximum use by individuals and groups. The play area should be conducive to individual as well as group use. There should be opportunities for numerous individual and group decisions regarding the activities to be pursued alone or together. There should be no need to wait in line for turns to use the equipment.

Year-round Use

The play area should be usable all year, regardless of the weather. There is no such thing as bad weather; there are only people improperly dressed for the various weather conditions.

5

Natural Topographical Features

NATURAL GEOLOGICAL FORMATIONS or topographical features of the play site should be used and capitalized upon for a quality play environment. In cases where a site has not yet been selected, the topography of various areas under consideration should be an important criterion for final determination of the site. When a play area has been in existence for a long time, and when the site is devoid of interesting and worthwhile natural features and formations, efforts to improve the area should include plans to restore or create topographical features.

Hills, Mounds, and Moguls

Small hills should be left on the site; or, if the area was bulldozed flat in the past, they should be restored. Mounds and moguls (ski hill term denoting man-made mounds on the large ski slope) are also desirable features. The entire play area should include sloping and flat terrain, from gentle grades to steep 45- to 60-degree slopes. Youngsters will use sleds, cardboard boxes, saucers, and skis to slide down these hills and slopes. They will run up and down them, too. They will lie down and roll to the bottom of grassy slopes. This kind of terrain can also be used for certain games.

Ponds

Children love water and ponds of all sizes, including the lowly mud puddle. Aquatic experiences are important to youngsters because such experiences contribute to the development of the tactile sense, as well as to a number of outdoor skills. Ponds should be provided on play area sites for ice skating and sliding in the winter season, and also ice fishing if the size of the pond is sufficient to allow stocking with fish. At other times of the year ponds will be used for wading, sailing toy boats, skipping flat stones, fishing (even with "pretend" gear—no hooks and bait), casting practice, and other activities suggested in Chapter 7.

Streams and Creeks

Streams and creeks will be used for many of the same purposes as ponds. Some additional activities are rafting and boating (given appropriate age groups), constructing bridges and dams, and the very exciting activity of pole vaulting across the width of such a body of water.

Boulders

Children love to climb over boulders, jump from them, stand upon them and view the surrounding area, and sometimes use them as part of a fort. Most boulders and large rocks can be used to good advantage.

Ravines

Ravines should be preserved or constructed so that youngsters will be able to climb in and out of them, construct bridges over them, jump across them, and make forts, caves, and hideouts by building roofs on them. Children also enjoy digging in ravines.

Trees, Bushes, and Shrubs

Shrubs, trees, and bushes have numerous purposes. They have physical value because they provide things for children to climb on; divide certain land areas from other areas (a busy street, for example); protect youngsters from wind, rain, and hot sun; reduce noise levels, especially in urban areas; act as snow fences; provide oxygen, which is particularly important in locales with heavy air pollution; and attract birds and small animals, sometimes providing homes for wildlife.

They also have great psychological value. A tree seems to make a home for a human being. It seems to provide comfort and security to humans. Youngsters and adults seek out and gravitate towards trees when they are outdoors. They like to sit under them, lean against them, and lie at their roots to read, talk, and eat. Furthermore, bushes and shrubs, as well as trees, provide little places in which children may hide, secret places where they can't be seen, but where they can reflect and dream and just be still. And finally, trees, bushes, and shrubs beautify an outdoor play area. Youngsters, just as much as, if not more than adults, love beauty and attractiveness. Creative outdoor play areas in inner cities, with careful planting of trees, shrubs, and bushes, can provide psychological resting places or havens. They provide much-needed respite.

Cliffs and Rock Outcroppings

Natural formations such as cliffs and rock outcroppings should be left intact wherever they are found. They add to the beauty and interesting appearance of an area, and youngsters will utilize them for a variety of purposes, including climbing and jumping.

Large Open Spaces

Relatively flat large open spaces are a necessity for every creative outdoor play area. They are particularly valuable for running and running games. Today's children, especially those in urban areas, need room for running. Running is probably the most characteristic motor skill in which children and youth engage. Yet the structure of many cities and neighborhoods almost suppresses it. Youngsters need big areas or long stretches of land on which to race and to play their favorite running games, as well as skip, ride bikes, sail kites, and throw balls. Some of these open spaces should be grassy; others should be of concrete or asphalt or both, with courts, lines, and circles marked upon them.

Paths, Trails, and Walkways

Paths, trails, and walkways should be interspersed throughout the creative outdoor play area for various purposes. In large play areas they can be used for hiking, leading youngsters from one nature highlight to another. They may be used as bicycle or tricycle trails, depending upon the overall size of the site. For handicapped children, particularly crippled and blind youngsters, the paths should have special features such as handrails, guide ropes, and ramps instead of steps. The paths and trails youngsters walk can be designed to motivate actions other than just walking; some pathways can be constructed to stimulate jumping or hopping; some may be constructed for perceptual-motor "patterning."

Surfaces

Creative outdoor play areas should contain a variety of surfaces for various purposes. Different kinds of surfaces contribute to the development of tactile perception, especially if youngsters are sometimes allowed to go barefoot. There should be surfaces and areas of sand, small smooth gravel, tough natural grass, blacktop or asphalt, outdoor carpeting, imitation turf, shredded tree bark, shredded wood, and tall weeds. Surfaces should be in harmony with a location and the play equipment located there. Soft surfaces should be selected for places where climbing equipment is positioned. A furrowed soil area should be considered for digging, raking, burying things, and such. A rail fence might be used to separate it from the remainder of the play area.

Other Considerations

Creative outdoor play areas may be large or small. An important thing to remember is that a small space seems large to young children. With careful designing, planting, construction, and positioning of equipment, a small play area will be perceived by youngsters as a great outdoor place.

In some cases it may be appropriate to include flower gardens on the play site. Youngsters might participate in their planting and care. They might also participate in the autumn planting of flower bulbs including tulips, crocuses, and daffodils.

Wherever possible or feasible, natural plant and tree materials which might be utilized by children for future projects should be planted. For example, willow trees might be planted in low spots on the site and used in the future for making willow whistles. The site itself then will provide some of the natural materials for children's play.

6

Creative
Play
Equipment

General Considerations

WHEN A CLASS OF INNER CITY elementary school youngsters were transported to the "country" for a day-long field trip, the children were delighted. For most, it was their very first trip out of the city. They were excited about the prospect of visiting a dairy farm and learning about milking cows, animal babies, and farm activities. When the school bus pulled up at their destination, the children flooded through its doors into the country outdoors. Much to the surprise of their teacher, however, instead of rushing towards the barns and farm animals, the entire group threw themselves down upon the top of a freshly mown, sweet smelling, and soft grassy hilltop, and rolled all the way to its bottom!

Simple, natural, and inexpensive.   Simple things are often the most fun and best loved by children. The most expensive pieces of play equipment are often ignored in favor of natural and inexpensive things like rail fences and cardboard boxes. Observation of children in the outdoors, when no traditional playground equipment is present, reveals some of the activities they love best—climbing and walking up on the tops of fences and stone walls, swinging and hanging from ropes and grape vines, climbing trees, and jumping ditches. Equipment for play areas need not be sophisticated or expensive. Children and youth provide many clues to the kind of equipment they like best. If these are not heeded, a school play area, such as the $13,000 fiberglass and steel playground with which the author is familiar, may be developed. The $13,000 equipment is rarely used; the children who attend that school would rather play in the little wooded area adjacent to the school site. Children don't use play equipment just because it's there.

Unlimiting and interpretable.   By its very nature, equipment often dictates to children and youth exactly how it shall be used. This is true of traditional iron and steel play equipment, which is extremely limiting in terms of what youngsters can do with it. The play activities of children should not be prescribed. Equipment ought to be such that youngsters will be able to interpret for themselves how they will use it. It ought to pose many alternatives for play activities. It should stimulate imagination and creativity. It ought to be freeing instead of limiting.

Children perceive things differently from adults. Youngsters don't use play equipment or play things as adults expect and intend them to be used. They use objects in their environments in unique ways, ways which will satisfy their needs and interests. While adults view some things as having one or possibly two purposes, youngsters see many purposes in them. A fence, for example, to children, has several uses, while most adults would limit its utility.

Moveable and/or adaptable. Much of the equipment in a play area should be moveable and changeable. Youngsters like to carry and rearrange things; they enjoy variety. They should be able to make and remake their play areas. Some pieces of play equipment ought to allow for alterations in physical location as well as in actual substance. The equipment should also be changeable when certain pieces no longer meet children's needs and interests. Equipment should be dismantled and reconstructed into something children will utilize, or removed from the play area altogether. In addition, equipment should be moveable in order to create "play stations," if desired. These play stations are gatherings of particular pieces of equipment deemed most appropriate for the needs and interests of certain age groups; or, they are groupings of equipment which contribute most to certain kinds of skills or activities, such as climbing skills or dramatic play.

Providing for large and small muscle action. Equipment should provide for big muscle movements of youngsters; it also should allow opportunities for fine muscle coordination and movement, such as balancing, pounding nails, sculpturing clay, and other manipulative activities. Equipment should be varied in size, shape, and complexity.

In addition, equipment should be such that children's bodies do the moving. Equipment which move children in a way in which they have to exert very little muscle action is poor equipment, if physical development and fitness are of concern.

Contributing to perceptual-motor development. Equipment should make a significant contribution to the perceptual-motor development of youngsters by providing opportunities for "patterning," spinning, balancing, rhythmic action, and other skills. It should be composed of varying textures, so that the tactile sense is developed. Tactile exploration of surroundings with all body parts is especially important to preschoolers. Aquatic experiences and barefoot play contribute to this kind of development, and equipment should provide opportunities for such.

Attractive. Equipment should have eye appeal for youngsters. They love colorful things. Gray, beige, black, brown, and army green are unattractive colors to children and youth. Unfortunately these colors characterize traditional play equipment. Where bright yellows and force-ful, earthy reds are used, children's interest in equipment is heightened.[1] Primary colors provide a freshness to a play area, and contrast well with the surrounding green of plants, trees, and grass.

Description of Equipment

In the following pages individual pieces of equipment are listed ac-cording to their major purposes and contributions. A number of them are presented visually in the pages of illustrations interspersed in the text. The ideas offered are not exhaustive. The reader's imagination and the creative thinking of youngsters who will use the equipment in creative outdoor play areas will expand the realm of play possibilities.

Most play equipment can be placed in the following categories: (1) dramatic play; (2) climbing; (3) jumping, leaping, and hopping; (4) swinging and hanging; (5) balance; (6) coordination—"patterning"; (7) throwing; (8) running, galloping, and skipping; (9) construction; (10) drawing, painting, and sculpturing; (11) other purposes. It should be noted that an individual piece of equipment may often be used for more than one purpose. In the following pages, multipurpose pieces of equip-ment will be listed under one category only, that of the most significant contribution.

Equipment for Dramatic Play

- Culverts brightly painted and positioned vertically or horizontally or both, sometimes grouped to resemble animals, insects, or worms.
- Culverts completely buried horizontally in a hill or mound to make a tunnel.
- Culverts positioned vertically and partly buried in the ground to make a "foxhole."
- Two culverts positioned horizontally on the surface of the ground and joined with a 150-degree elbow to make a tunnel.
- Old vehicles brightly painted and secured in the ground, including an Amish buggy, trolley or streetcar, antique touring automobile, skimobile, fire engine, tractor, stagecoach, propeller-driven air-plane, and a Conestoga wagon.
- "Dug-out" canoes made of logs cut in half lengthwise and hol-lowed out.
- Metal slides, curved and straight, laid at ground level on small hills and mounds.

[1] Alexander Grey, "Creative Learning in Children's Playgrounds," *Childhood Education,* May, 1969, p. 496.

— Old boats brightly painted and secured to the ground, including a sailboat, iceboat, aluminum or fiberglass canoe, rowboat, and lifeboat (with seating planks which could be used as a seating area for parents, senior citizens, and others).

— "Space rocket" built from logs and a metal waste container.

— A large dead tree positioned horizontally on the ground, trimmed, notched, and painted to resemble a dragon or other animal.

— Train engine constructed from a wooden crate, drainage tile, and culvert.

— Canvas tents of various shapes and sizes.

— Wooden rafts in streams or ponds, anchored at water level or secured, so that they are partly sunken or submerged.

— Large modular hollow boxes made of plywood with one side open, forming cubes and pyramids.

— Strong corrugated cardboard appliance boxes.

— Tarpaulins, blankets, and old fashioned clothing.

— Old steering wheels.

— Old horse saddle mounted upon a log, stump, or other kind of base. VIEW ZOO

— Wooden tents (A-frames).

— Lean-to "garage" for parking tricycles and bicycles.

— Puppet theater or stage.

— "Horse and cattle corrals" made of logs or boards (for climbing and balancing also).

— Old railroad caboose or boxcar brightly painted and used as a playhouse, crafts shop, tool storage shed, or art gallery.

— Indian teepees constructed from wooden poles or logs and wood slabs or sheets of plywood.

— Indian teepes constructed from bamboo poles and large plastic sheets.

— Wooden barrels of different sizes.

— Tree houses of one or more levels built around a living tree trunk or another kind of supporting structure.

— Water sprinklers with spouts buried in ground, attached to pieces of equipment, or hidden in walls (to trickle into wading pools).

— Wooden boxes and packing crates.

— Wooden and rope bridges built over streams and ravines.

— Pioneer log cabin.

— Settlers' fort made from logs.

— Pioneer sod house.

— Airplanes, automobiles, segmented worms, animals, and trains made from solid or hollow logs of varying lengths and circumferences, trimmed and joined together.

— Incan or Egyptian type pyramids made of bricks or concrete blocks (for climbing also).

— Medieval style castle made of bricks, fieldstone, or concrete blocks.

— Greco-Roman amphitheater with a stage constructed from bricks, stone, or concrete blocks.

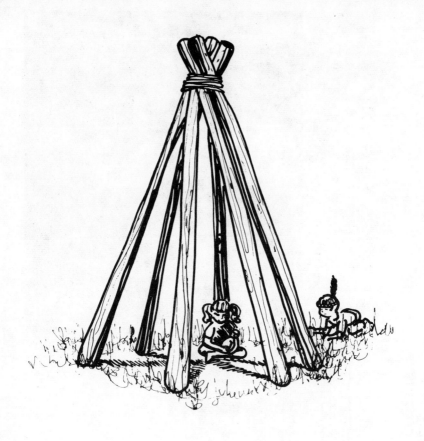

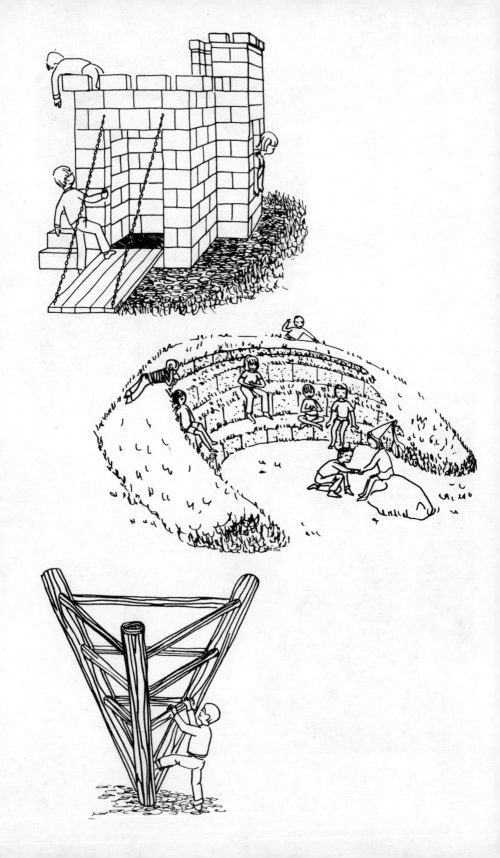

— Stream with a manmade waterfall and pool in which to splash.
— Playhouses built on one or more levels.
— Wooden platform built above ground in a living tree or around a utility pole, with a "fireman's pole" for climbing and sliding.
— "Look-out tower" made of logs (for climbing also).

Equipment for Climbing

— Culverts positioned vertically with holes cut for handgrips and footholds.
— Concrete slabs, several feet wide and high, 3 to 6 feet thick, set vertically in the ground with holes cut for handgrips and footholds.
— Logs and wooden utility poles of varying heights positioned vertically with notches cut for handgrips and footholds.
— Pillars made of cement blocks alternately laid horizontally and vertically.
— Picket, rail, plank, and log fences of various heights and lengths, curved and straight (for jumping and balancing also).
— Large dead trees with big branches trimmed, bark stripped off, and horizontally positioned on the ground (for jumping and balancing also).
— Wooden telephone and electric wire "spools" (for jumping also).
— Dead debarked trees with strong trimmed branches set vertically in the ground, singly or in groups, to make a "climbing forest."
— Varying lengths of utility poles and railroad ties laid crosswise upon each other in alternate layers (for jumping and balancing also).
— Railroad ties secured crosswise upon each other in orderly layers to form an open pyramid.
— Boulder piles and fieldstone mounds (fieldstones might be mortared for greater stability).
— Walls of brick, rock, cement blocks, or concrete of different lengths, shapes, and heights, with bricks, blocks, and rocks jutting out and holes left in various places (for jumping and balancing also).
— Knotted ropes hanging from tree limbs or other supporting structures (for hanging and swinging also).
— Tree stumps of varying heights left in the ground; some of the taller ones might have ladders attached vertically to their sides.
— Stairways or staircases constructed of railroad ties, log sections, log discs, and boulders, built on hills, mounds, and inclines (for jumping and running also).
— Rope cargo nets suspended from or stretched between poles, logs, or thrown over an old iron swing frame.
— Large piles of utility poles of varying lengths laid in different directions, and bolted together for stability (resembling a pile of giant toothpicks) (for balancing also).
— Sections of utility poles or logs secured vertically in the ground.

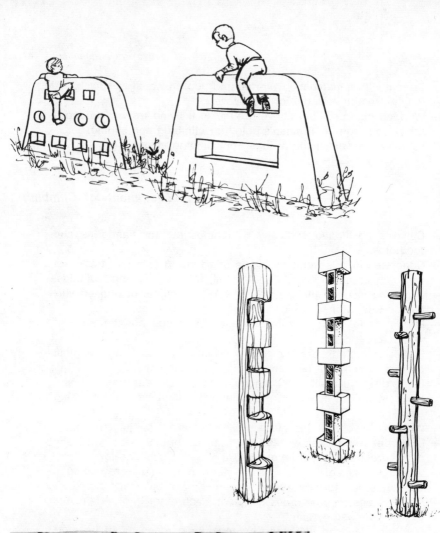

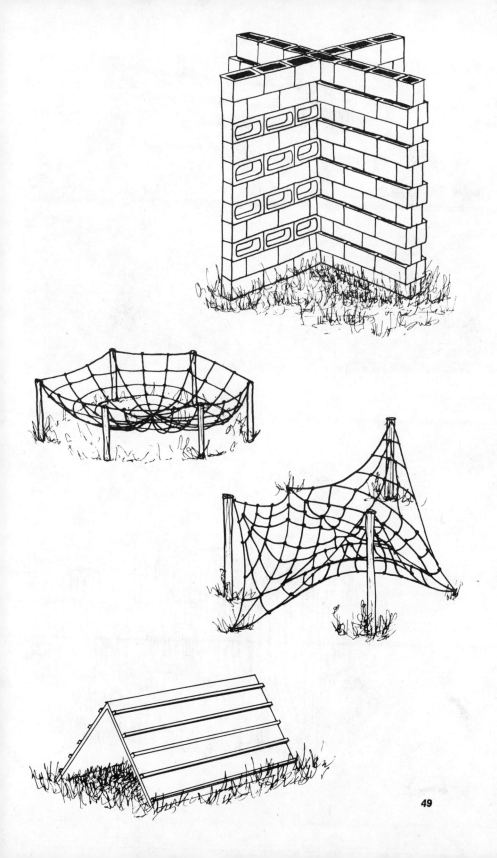

with large dowels inserted every 6 to 10 feet for handgrips and footholds.

— Plywood sheets joined to form A-frame structures with 2 to 3 feet wide wooden "ribs" (boards) attached horizontally at intervals of 6 to 10 feet.

— Long wooden ladders positioned horizontally several feet above the ground and extending for 15, 20, or 40 feet, supported as necessary by vertical poles.

— Smooth wooden or steel poles (old flag poles could be utilized), 10 to 20 feet high, positioned vertically in the ground.

— Utility poles of different lengths set vertically in the ground at varying distances from each other, linked by horizontal steel bars, wooden poles or logs, ropes, cargo nets, or a combination of the preceding.

— Railroad ties placed upon each other at irregular angles and bolted where they cross.

— Wooden "stile" hinged at the top, with an adjustable chain connecting the lower portions of each side.

— Tall carpenter's horses (sawhorses) with wooden slats nailed horizontally at intervals of 3 to 10 feet on all four sides.

— Two precast concrete home front porch stoops positioned back to back, or a similar structure built of logs, planks, or railroad ties.

— Logs of varying lengths, 6 feet and less, set vertically in the ground side by side.

— Utility pole or large log "mountain" with poles or logs placed vertically in the ground so that they touch, with the ones on the outside of the "mountain" very short and the ones towards the middle progressively taller.

Equipment for Jumping, Leaping, and Hopping

— Boulders placed in a shallow stream so that their tops protrude.

— "Spring pads" made of wooden planks.

— Tree stumps left in the ground, sawed off at various heights, and painted brightly.

— Tiles of concrete and clay set vertically in the ground, and "capped" with concrete or wooden discs to resemble mushrooms.

— Automobile, motorcycle, tractor, and truck tires vertically positioned or laid flat on the ground.

— High-jump apparatus made of two thin wooden boards or poles vertically positioned in the ground approximately 5 or 6 feet apart. The boards or poles should be at least 6 feet in height. On each, nails or pegs should be placed at ½" intervals from the top to within 6 inches above the ground. A bamboo pole or rope with weighted ends will serve as a cross bar.

Equipment for Swinging and Hanging

- Low and high "parallel bars" of wooden poles or steel bars.
- Horizontal climber of logs and wooden dowels.
- Burlap sack filled with foam rubber bits, tied to the end of a long rope which is suspended from a tree limb or other kind of support.
- Single rope suspended from a tree limb or other kind of support at the edge of a pond, so that the swinger can release over the pond and fall into the water.
- Narrow wooden or steel bar, approximately 3 feet in length, positioned horizontally and suspended by two ropes hung from a tree limb or other kind of support (trapeze type swing).
- Automobile or motorcycle tires in vertical or horizontal positions hung by ropes or chains from a tree limb or other kind of supporting structure.
- Swings with leather or rubber strap seats.
- Sturdy grape vines.
- Dead tree positioned vertically in the ground with low horizontal limbs.

Equipment for Developing Balance

- Wooden stilts.
- Logs, 6 to 8 feet in length, for logrolling on land.
- Low, straight, and contoured walls made of bricks, rocks, concrete, or concrete blocks.
- Poles or logs placed across the width of a stream.
- Logs, 4 by 4's, 2 by 2's, or railroad ties, laid end to end on the ground forming straight or angled lines.
- Wooden carpenter's horses (sawhorses).
- Logs, utility poles, and railroad ties horizontally positioned 2 and 4 feet above the ground with the ends mounted on stumps, cement blocks, or steel pipes.
- Wooden ladders positioned horizontally 1 to 3 feet above the ground with ends resting on low brick walls or other kinds of support.
- High balance beams made of 4 by 4 timbers.
- Steel railroad rails laid side by side on the ground for 20 feet or more.

Equipment and Surface Markings
for Developing Coordination and "Patterning"

— Wooden discs, 3, 6, 8, 10, 12, and 14 feet wide made by sawing crosswise logs of different circumferences. The discs should be positioned flat on the ground in varying distances from each other. They may number as many as 150 and be placed in curving patterns, positioned in and around trees and other objects, or be used as a "challenge course." Youngsters could jump, leap, hop, or step from one to another.

— Flat rocks, bricks placed together to form squares and rectangles, or concrete blocks set into the ground at varying distances from each other to form patterns and paths for jumping, running, hopping, and leaping.

— Short logs of variable heights set into the ground at even or uneven distances from each other to be used as "stepping stumps."

— Hopscotch patterns, shuffleboard diagrams, marbles' circles, four-square courts and similar markings for other games painted on concrete or asphalt surfaces, or marked in wet cement. In addition, a variety of circles, rectangles, squares, right and left footprint patterns, and wavy lines may be painted or marked on hard surfaces.

Equipment for Throwing

— Animals and various geometric shapes cut out of plywood sheets, painted brightly, and mounted on posts or hung from tree limbs to be used as targets for snowballs, rocks, and balls.

— Walls made of bricks, concrete, cement blocks, or wood, and differing in length and height, against which to bounce and bat balls. Targets may be painted on the walls.

— Low basketball backboards and baskets.

— "Hoola" and barrel hoops mounted on poles at varying heights.

— Targets painted on the outside of buildings where there are no windows.

— Large bullseye type target (concentric circles) painted on asphalt or concrete ground surface (similar to clout archery target).

— Vertically positioned backboards with holes of varying sizes through which different objects can be thrown.

— Ground pits of different sizes into which balls, marbles, and other objects can be rolled or thrown.

— Cardboard and wooden barrels, kegs, and boxes placed on ground into which objects may be thrown.

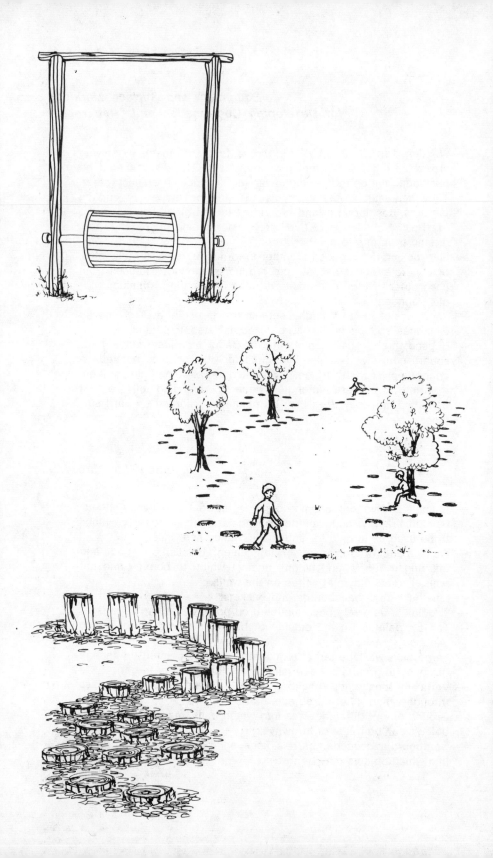

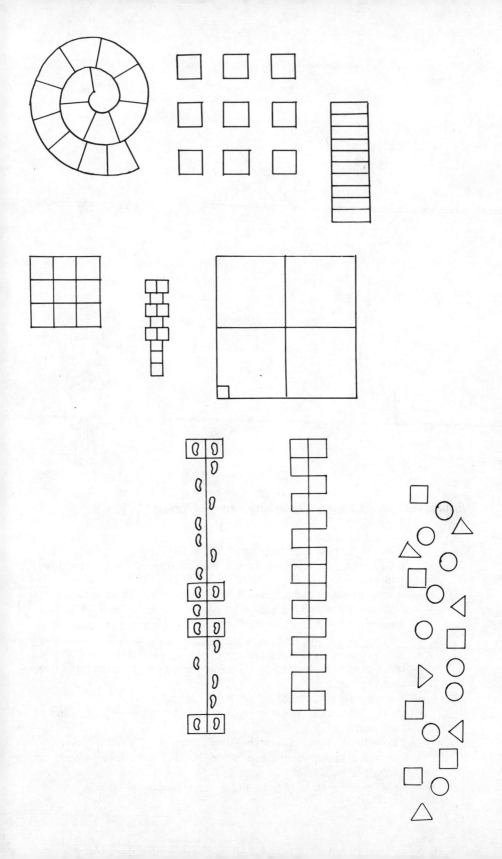

Equipment for Running, Galloping, and Skipping

— "Challenge courses" composed of a variety of equipment pieces—logs, sand pits, stiles, vertically and horizontally positioned tires, and others.

— Ramps made of asphalt, wood, brick, concrete blocks, or earth.

— Distance markings indicating 50 yards, 100 yards, and other measurements painted on asphalt and concrete surfaces or marked by poles or signs in grassy areas.

— Maze created by shrub plantings or a wooden slab fence. A foot or more of space left open at the bottom will allow children lost in the maze to "escape."

— Running broad jump approach area and pit.

— Oval "junior size" running track made of asphalt or other kind of hard surface.

— Zig zag lines painted on asphalt or concrete.

— Footsteps resembling those made by galloping feet painted on asphalt or concrete.

— Poles positioned in ground similar to a slalom ski course.

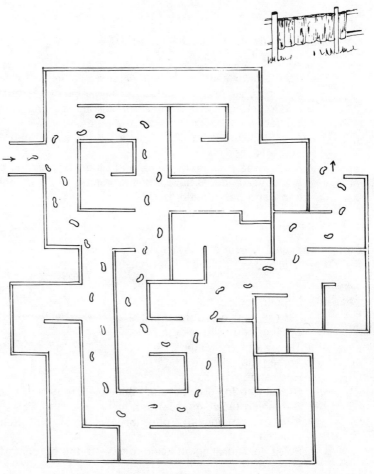

Equipment for Developing Construction Skills

— Logs varying in circumference and length, from 1 or 2 to 12 feet.
— Logs and planks of varying lengths notched on the ends.
— Wooden discs 3 feet or so in width, sawed crosswise from logs.
— Boards, planks, railroad ties, corrugated metal sheets, lumber, old doors, plastic panels, styrofoam sheets and boxes, and grapevine posts.
— Bricks, flagstones, rocks, and cement blocks.
— Wheelbarrows, carpenter's horses, hammers, saws, rope, straight wire, chicken wire, and ladders.
— Bamboo poles, branches, tall weeds, and rushes.
— Flags, canvas, heavy plastic sheets, and cloth.
— Buggy, wagon, and automobile wheels.

Equipment for Drawing, Painting, and Sculpturing

— Sand pits or sand piles with water available for wetting the sand.
— Soft logs, such as Ponderosa or sugar pine, perhaps to be made into totem poles, for group and individual carving activities.
— Outdoor chalkboards with clips to hold paper.
— A wall designated as the "painting wall" to be continually painted and repainted.
— A wall where flags, banners, and other decorations can be hung.
— A wall which could have a mural painted on it (through community effort and participation).

Equipment and Surface Markings for Other Purposes

— Rubber conical traffic markers.
— Asphalt and concrete trails, 2 or 3 feet wide, for bicycling, tricycling, and roller skating.
— Target archery range.
— Archery golf course.
— Horseshoe courts.
— Gravel pile for hunting and collecting pretty and unusual stones.
— Gardening tools—rakes, hoes, shovels, and trowels—of children's size, for use in sand piles or in a small cultivated section of ground.
— Poles for hurdling in sand pits and for hurdling the width of streams.

— Shallow cement wading pool structure for tricycling and roller skating in warm months, and ice skating in cold months (when filled with water).
— Painted markings on asphalt and concrete surfaces including circles, rectangles, squares, and courts for various games and sports.
— Sundial made of pipe and concrete.
— Scale likeness of the sun and planets painted on a concrete or asphalt surface.
— Large map of the United States or a single state painted on a concrete or asphalt surface.
— Various kinds of animal tracks imprinted in concrete.

7

Examples of Comprehensive Play Areas

BECAUSE IT MIGHT BE DIFFICULT to perceive a creative outdoor play area composed of many of the topographical features and pieces of equipment described in the preceding chapters, several layouts are provided here. Each of the play area sketches is intended to show: a variety of categories of equipment, surfaces, surface markings, and topographical features; varying acreages; play possibilities for all ages, preschoolers through youths; aesthetically pleasing designs. Also shown are "self-contained" sections of larger play areas which could be built first, developed later, eliminated completely, or constructed as completed play areas on tiny pieces of land which would not be large enough to accommodate anything larger. As can be seen, the "self-contained" sections are usually separated to a certain extent from the rest of the play area by trees, bushes, low walls, fences, boulders, or surfacing. All of these tend to reduce youngsters' haphazard "traffic" across the entire acreage, which is a factor in promoting safety.

Because children and youth love self-challenge and competition from others, "challenge courses" (obstacle courses) are desirable as self-contained sections within total play areas. Where only a small piece of land is available for a creative outdoor play area, a challenge course might encompass the entire land area. Challenge courses should be comprised of a variety of equipment pieces, all demanding different movements and skills.

Key:

1. Concrete surface with painted markings for games and "patterning"
2. Boulders
3. Wooden posts of varying heights
4. Vertical culverts
5. Utility post, log and pole climber
6. Rail fence
7. Low log fence
8. Row boat
9. Stumps
10. Log with horse saddle
11. Log train
12. Log animals
13. Horizontal ladders
14. Horizontal culverts
15. Tire swings
16. Sand pit
17. Painting wall

Play Area II

Size: three or four acres; Location: school site

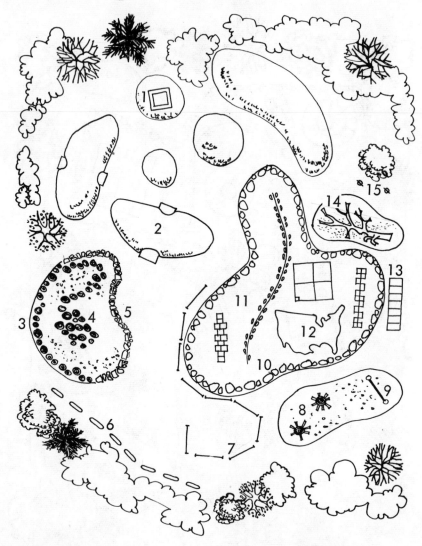

Key:

1. Mogul with lookout platform
2. Mound with culvert tunnel

3. Low wooden discs
4. Short log climber

5. Low fieldstone wall
6. Automobile tires set vertically
7. Low railroad tie balance beams
8. Tall utility pole climbers
9. Long rope climber

10. Flat rock "stepping stones"
11. Concrete surface with painted markings for games and "patterning"
12. Painted map of United States
13. Low horizontal balancer of planks and railroad ties
14. Dead tree climber
15. Targets for throwing

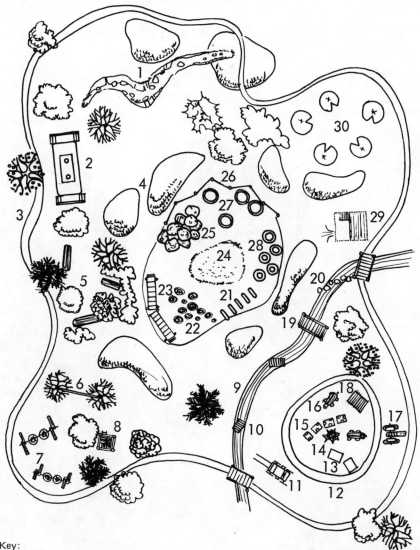

Key:

1. Ravine
2. Train caboose
3. Bicycle trail
4. Mounds
5. Quiet area with logs for sitting
6. Trapeze swing
7. Tire swings
8. Lookout tower
9. Stream
10. Raft

11. Amish buggy
12. Tricycle track
13. Horizontal culverts
14. Stump
15. Segmented worm of horizontal culverts
16. Log animals
17. Tractor
18. Wooden A-frame tent
19. Bridge
20. Boulders

21. Automobile tires set vertically
22. Post climber
23. Horizontal ladders
24. Sand pit
25. Boulder pile
26. Log fence
27. Vertical culverts
28. Tractor tires laid flat
29. Settlers' fort
30. Indian teepee village

67

8

Children's Gardens

AMONG THE EXCITING NEW DEVELOPMENTS in children's play areas are children's gardens, sometimes referred to as Children's Adventure Gardens. A number of municipal parks, schools, school systems, citizens' clubs, and agencies provide children and youth with opportunities to work in the soil. For many youngsters, especially those who live in urban areas, gardening is a brand-new experience, foreign to both them and their parents. It is an experience which returns to the children not only real "products" in the form of vegetables, fruits, and flowers, but also excitement, fun, and joy. This is true not only for preschoolers and elementary school children involved in such programs, but for more mature and sophisticated secondary school youth.

Value

Besides providing children with happy and thrilling experiences, gardening opportunities provide prevocational education opportunities. As a result, even city youngsters involved in gardening and related activities often pursue adult careers in horticulture, agriculture, or related professions.

The frequent concomitant involvement of local community people, such as the local garden club, provides meaningful cooperation and communication between people of differing ages.

Children's gardens are little spots of beauty which have the potential to make a significant impact upon outdoor community beautification.

Gardening helps children to gain an understanding in the academic areas of science, social studies, and economics. They learn about the rural living experiences of their "country cousins" and their forefathers; they gain knowledge about the economic survival of Americans from the first pioneers to present-day citizens; they become acquainted with the history, age-old superstitions, and true physical benefits of various plants.

That vegetables are not manufactured in grocery stores is a startling concept learned by many city youngsters.

Youngsters acquire skills for their present and future leisure time pursuits.

70

Children's gardens help children and youth understand difficult concepts such as overpopulation. They can see what overpopulation does to growing plants, and apply or transfer that understanding to human beings.

The total plant growing cycle—seeds to seedlings to maturity and fruit production to decay to rebirth from self-produced seeds—helps youngsters to gain a new perspective on the human life cycle. To understand the full cycle of sowing seeds to the eventual harvesting of mature plants provides children with a complete experience in learning. The child starts something, then sees its culmination. This kind of experience is an infrequent occurrence in the lives of today's children; most of their experiences at home, in church, and in school are fragmentary and partial.

Finally, gardening provides youngsters with enjoyment and stimulation. As their plants grow, so do their interest, awe, curiosity, and motivation.

Types

Gardens vary greatly in types. Children may raise perennial or annual flowers. They may have wildflower gardens. Their flower gardens may be specialized: Shakespeare, rose, dahlia, cactus, among others. They may plant bulb beds. Children's gardens may be vegetable gardens with as many as thirty or forty varieties including corn, lettuce, green beans, radishes, onions, tomatoes, squash, eggplant, chives, carrots, cabbage, turnips, peppers, parsnips, broccoli, asparagus, peas, and potatoes. Some have herb gardens, wildlife attraction gardens composed of plants such as sunflower and corn, and beds of plants which will make natural dyes. Youngsters may raise exotic flowers and plants such as orchids. They may, in addition to their outdoor gardens, have a small greenhouse. Some children develop experimental plots in which they test out varying kinds of fertilizer on plants, carry out crossbreeding experiments, and develop new varieties. For many city youngsters who live in apartment buildings or houses without yards, rooftop gardens and window box gardens may be most appropriate or desirable.

Size

The size of children's gardens varies with the age level of the children involved and with the availability of land. For preschool children and for those in early elementary school, a plot 4 by 6 feet will suffice for each individual child. Older youngsters of later elementary and junior high school ages can take care of plots 10 by 15 feet or so. Many schools and school systems which offer gardening to their students give 24 by 30 foot plots or one-quarter to one-half of an acre per classroom (20 to 30 students). Often there is also a communal plot provided for the combined use of several classrooms in which plants such as pumpkins and squash are grown. Sometimes, instead of providing each individual child with a single piece of land for his garden, pairs of children are given the responsibility for one plot. In any case, size allotment will also depend upon the means of cultivating the gardens. If mechanical equipment is available, such as a rototiller, plots can be larger than those in which all work is to be done by youngsters with hoes and rakes. Marking off plots with string and stakes is essential in designating the exact location of property for which a child is responsible.

Organization

Preparation.   This may begin for the normal outdoor growing season during the winter and spring months in indoor and outdoor settings. Children may grow seeds indoors for seedlings to be transplanted outdoors later. This is especially easy to do if youngsters have access to a greenhouse. Some elementary and secondary schools have greenhouses as part of the school building. Sometimes children who are interested in gardening are provided during the winter and spring months with a "gardencraft" program in which they learn about the planning and management of flower and vegetable gardens. Preparation for the outdoor season can also include the drawing of diagrams for proper seed and seedling placement. During the preparatory months children can learn garden-related crafts, such as making root boxes, birdhouses, coldframes, and hotbeds. Sending for mail-order seed and garden supply catalogs, studying them, and then ordering seeds and plants are exciting activities in which youngsters may engage. Seeds and seedlings may be started outdoors in the early spring months by using coldframes and hotbeds.

Spading or plowing.   This stage is of critical importance in the growing of children's gardens. Some youngsters, especially older youths who are considerably stronger than elementary and preschool children, may gain the most satisfaction in preparing their plots by hand spading. Plowing by tractor or rototilling may be more appropriate for many. Most youngsters will enjoy doing the final preparation of the plots—the raking—by hand. That is followed by measuring and staking off rows.

Planting of seeds and seedlings.   This is one of the highlights of the entire gardening process. While older youngsters should be allowed to choose the kinds of plants they wish to raise, preschoolers may be given a "Garden Adventure Kit" containing one tomato plant, one packet of green beans, one packet of zinnias, several gladiola bulbs, and a little fertilizer. Flower, vegetable, or fruit seeds and seedlings may be planted in conventional rows, or placed in special ways so that they become contributors to the play and fantasy world of youngsters. For example, pole beans may be planted to grow and cover a teepee made of wooden poles or climb an arbor forming a darkened tunnel. Cucumbers and other vine type plants can be trained in similar ways; they might be planted to climb the branches of a dead tree, thus making a "vegetable tree." Watermelons might be planted within a patch of corn to form a watermelon and corn jungle. Giant corn may be planted to make a corn forest. A "Charlie Brown" giant pumpkin patch might be planted. Root boxes with plastic or glass sides, resembling aquariums, are sometimes planted to show children how slowly and in what ways different plants grow. Planting activities may continue over a period of several months, because some plants, such as lettuce, mature early and may be put in the ground before the danger of frost is past; others, such as turnips, mature late and should be planted in mid summer.

Care of growing plants. Children may wish to conduct experiments showing the difference between thinned and unthinned plants, fertilized and unfertilized plants, weeded and unweeded plants. Cultivating can be done easily by hoe. The best part of caring for growing plants, in the minds of many children, is watering. Youngsters love to water their gardens.

Harvesting. Fruit, vegetable, and flower harvesting is probably the most exciting part of gardening for young and old. The harvests belong entirely to the children. They will enjoy harvesting crops over a period of several weeks, as some plants mature early, and others late in the growing season. After corn is picked, corn shock forts and hideouts may be constructed, providing additional fun for youngsters.

Produce

The harvested produce from school gardens is shared among the children. Sometimes a group of students and their teacher will themselves prepare a meal of their own garden produce. Many of the vegetables may have never been eaten by the youngsters; consequently, some children find themselves enjoying food they heretofore believed they disliked.

The highlight of harvest time for many children is a "Parent Night Buffet," featuring crops the youngsters have grown. The pride of the children at such an event is indescribable.

At the autumn conclusion of some gardening programs, a "Children's Garden Fair" is held, allowing youngsters to exhibit their prized fruit, vegetables, and flowers. This is often followed by a "Garden Awards Program." At this time each child exhibits a product and receives an achievement award or recognition for his efforts.

An annual "Giant Pumpkin Contest" may be held for those young people who have chosen to grow pumpkins. This may be held in conjunction with a pumpkin carving contest near Halloween time.

Children and youth who enjoy raising flowers may be given flower arranging instruction by a local garden club or knowledgeable adult.

For some youngsters, entering produce in the county agricultural fair is a worthwhile and enjoyable activity.

Youngsters sometimes establish a little produce market to sell their flowers, vegetables and fruit. This helps them to understand agricultural economics; it also helps to provide funds for future garden programs.

Other Activities

Opportunities to make field trips to a city market are sometimes part of the youngsters' gardening experience. Many also enjoy opportunities to visit truck farms, florist shops and greenhouses, landscape farms, university horticulture, floriculture, and plant laboratories. For some, a conversation with a full time farmer is a new and enjoyable experience.

Frequently children and youth enjoy carrying out landscaping activities in conjunction with their gardening projects. The planning, mapping, and planting of an entire yard, park, courtyard, or school site is challenging to many. For others, simpler activities, such as building a wishing well or a little pond and waterfall to grace a small flower garden spot, bring enjoyment.

9

Children's
Farms

CHILDREN'S FARMS ARE AN EXCITING development in outdoor education and outdoor recreation. Since so many children live in urban areas and rarely get away from them, and since there are relatively few farms in the nation today (of those which still exist, the great majority are highly specialized—unlike the typical American farm of 25 or 40 years ago), there is a great need to preserve or restore some farms for the enjoyment and education of youngsters.

Benefits of our once rural culture have been lost. It is an unfortunate fact that many of today's children don't know that milk comes from cows, honey is made by bees, and bacon comes from hogs. Today's children should not be deprived of the experiences of touching a calf's velvety nose, perching on a barnyard fence, snuggling baby chicks close to their cheeks, smelling newly mown hay, flushing quail from a fence row, and seeing a family of pheasants cross a dirt road.

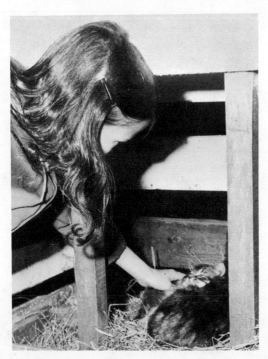

Children's farms are being developed throughout the country with the aid of school systems, municipal park and recreation departments, public recreation areas, and private enterprise. Almost nothing is as thrilling to citified children as a visit to a farm, particularly if the farm is well stocked with different kinds of animals and fowl, especially baby livestock and poultry.

Value

Children's farms provide urban youngsters the opportunities to experience the smells, sounds, and sights of a farm community. Children and youth learn how crops, such as wheat and corn, are planted, cultivated, and harvested; how livestock and poultry are born, bred, cared for, and fed. Children can experience actual farm work, including cleaning pens and stalls, repairing and painting farm equipment and fences, planting and harvesting crops, including baling hay and straw, and feeding fowl and animals. Sometimes children become involved in farm site improvement projects such as weeding, controlling soil and wind erosion, and planting trees. They learn homemaking practices, such as picking fruits and vegetables, then canning and freezing them; these experiences will be valuable when they as adults are heads of family units. Children's farms link the past with the present and afford youngsters opportunities to study a wide range of social studies.

Types

The character of a children's farm is determined by the overall purpose of the facility. Some farms are re-creations of centers of pioneer life or farms resembling those of the first half of the twentieth century. These farms are the most popular types and probably serve the interests of the greatest number and range of children and youth. Depending upon the region of the country in which they are located, the farms may be either typically midwestern (designed after the New England farms with barns attached to the farm houses), or southwestern or western (constructed of sod or adobe).

Some children's farms are modern, demonstrating all the latest agricultural practices and exhibiting the newest facilities. They may be specialized hog or cattle farms, or specific crop-raising farms only. These farms are enjoyed most by youth who are considering some form of modern agriculture as a future vocation.

There are a few fantasy farms for children in existence. Some are called "Old MacDonald's Farm" and are built around the themes of children's nursery rhymes and stories. A "Jack and Jill" well, the homes of the "Three Little Pigs," and other storybook characters and places are highlighted in fantasy farms.

Facilities

Physical facilities vary according to the type of farm. The following physical facilities are generally provided for children's enjoyment and learning.

— A *wood lot,* often called the "back forty," replete with wildflowers and trails.

— A *farm pond* for boating, rafting, wading, and stocked with pan fish for fishing.

— A *farm produce market* for the selling by children of vegetables and fruits grown at the farm.

— A *farm shop* for repairing harnesses and other farm equipment. Such a shop may also be used by children and youth as a crafts center in which they carve wood, sculpture clay, and engage in other handicrafts.

— A *root cellar* for the storage and preservation of vegetables and fruits, including potatoes, squash, and apples.

— A *blacksmith shop* for shodding farm horses and forging iron tools.

— A *working windmill* pumping water for livestock.

— A *well* and *hand pump.*

— A *maple sugaring shack* for boiling maple sap into syrup.

— A *farm wagon* providing youngsters with hay rides.

— A *farm buggy* for the experience of driving and riding a horse drawn vehicle.

— A *poultry house* for farm fowl and a *hatchery* for chicks.

— *Barns* sheltering horses and other animals; some include a "milking parlor" for cows, and a hay loft.

— An oldtime *farmhouse* or *pioneer log cabin home* with authentic furnishings of the period represented. Some have been adapted to provide dormitories or other overnight quarters and facilities for youngsters who wish to experience a twenty-four hour or longer stay on the farm.

— A *smokehouse* for curing farm produced hams, bacon, and sausage.

— A *grainery* for wheat, oats, or other farm grown grain.

— A *corncrib* for storing corn.

— A *silo* to make silage as feed for livestock.

— A *horse tank* filled by a working windmill.

— A *farmhouse vegetable garden* with a *scarecrow.*

— A *milkhouse* for preparing and storing milk.

— A variety of modern or pioneer *farm machinery* and *equipment* including a tractor, combine, plow, disc, harrow, grain elevator, steam engine.

Livestock

A variety of domestic farm animals and fowl are provided on children's farms. They usually include horses, milk cows, beef cattle, chickens, pigs, goats, sheep, ponies, ducks, swans, geese, donkeys, rabbits, guinea fowl, peacocks, mules, and turkeys. Personal contact with the domestic animals, which can be handled, is encouraged. Some farms raise bees and display the apiary in a farm orchard or other suitable location. Farm cats and dogs are to be considered significant inhabitants of the farm animal community.

Besides domestic animals, wild game birds and fur bearing animals are sometimes raised in pens and cages on the farm; these include pheasants, partridge, crows, quail, owls, deer, opossums, raccoons, ground hogs, and squirrels.

As is true on any farm, wild animals flourish in the woods, fields, and bodies of water. Children may glimpse, in their natural habitats, deer, squirrels, foxes, muskrats, ground hogs, owls, and pheasants.

Domestic livestock and fowl, penned and caged animals and birds

are often identified by signs bearing their scientific and informal names, children being the sources of many of the latter. Donated by the children of Fremont Elementary School, "Fremont" is a well-known donkey at the school's children's farm. Children and youth take great delight in making friends with domestic and wild animals by naming them.

It seems fair to say that springtime on the farm is the favorite season of most children. Present are animal babies of nearly every species, and not much is more appealing to the young of the human race!

Crops

Crops grown on any farm are those germane to that geographical area of the country. They may include some or all of the following: corn, wheat, oats, barley, buckwheat, sugar beets, alfalfa, timothy, and soybeans. In hilly country, farm conservation includes practices such as contour plowing and strip cropping.

Besides the aforementioned crops, farm produce may include honey from bees; milk, cheese, and butter from cows; beef, lamb, veal, and pork from livestock; and eggs from chickens. Apples, cherries, raspberries, currants, grapes, peaches, gooseberries, blueberries, plums, and strawberries grown in beds, vineyards, and orchards comprise a farm's important fruit crop. It is preferable to have dwarf fruit trees on a children's farm because of the ease with which youngsters may pick their own fruit and smell and investigate the blossoms.

Regular Events

Youngsters should be made aware of, and encouraged to participate in, certain events which take place regularly on a farm. These include gathering eggs from the hen house every morning, feeding the animals and fowl, and milking the cows morning and evening. There is an orderliness and regularity to these activities which children and youth appreciate.

Regular events often take place on a seasonal rather than daily basis. Because of their infrequent occurrence, they will be described as special events.

Special Facilities

Special facilities as part of a children's farm bring added enjoyment and excitement, as well as learning, to youngsters. The following are among the most significant:

— A *covered bridge* over a stream or creek which runs through farm property; the bridge should be a replica of those typical of some parts of the country.

— A *blacksmith shop* where children and youth see farm and household tools and implements being made and repaired.

— A *cheese factory* on a dairy farm where different kinds of cheeses are made periodically. This plant is especially appropriate in the dairy states of the nation.

— A *pioneer museum* housed in an old barn, a restored log cabin, or other suitable building. Pioneer agricultural equipment and old-time homemaking articles are displayed. Children are encouraged to touch, turn, open, put on, and move the "antiques."

— A *pioneer log cabin* or *log house,* restored and refurbished to show children and youth a glimpse of early America. Youngsters may be given the opportunity to cook and eat meals, sleep overnight, and use the structure as would their historical counterparts. The local or state historical society might play an important role in restoring and operating the log cabin or house and the aforementioned museum. Community people might be willing to donate antiques, when they know such goods will be cared for and used to benefit others.

— An old time *sawmill* placed near the "back forty," or woodlot. This is a fascinating structure, especially to older youth who might be allowed to help operate it.

— A restored *gristmill,* used to grind farm products.

— An old-time *general store,* stocked with articles typical of stores 40 or 80 years ago. This provides youngsters with many enjoyable learning experiences in social studies and economics.

— A *one-room schoolhouse,* a favorite of children and youth. One abandoned in the geographical region might be moved to the farm site, then restored to its original condition. Children, with or without adult supervision, may "play school" in the building, dressed in "period" clothing, and pretending to carry out the practices of earlier times.

— The restoration of an abandoned, but historically significant, *community church.* This would furnish another building of interest to youngsters.

— An old-time *post office* and *railroad depot,* potentially important elements in a child's understanding of the total operation of a farm.

The possibility of establishing a "Pioneer Life Center" or a "Rural Life Center," a combination of the usual farm equipment and procedures plus some of the special structures discussed previously, should be considered. For millions of children and youth who live in urban areas, such a center for play and learning could provide the most thrilling experiences of their lives.

Special Events

These are numerous at a children's farm. The type of event depends upon the nature of farm, its facilities, and its geographical location. The following activities may be offered:

— *Apple butter making* in the autumn, using apples grown on the farm, picked and "snitzed" [1] by children. An old-time family recipe, authentic copper kettle, and a long-handled wooden stirrer with cornhusk ties might be used. The butter should be cooked over an open fire on the farm property.

— *Cider production,* another autumn activity popular with youngsters. The cider should be made from apples grown on the farm.

— *Cornhusking bee*—an old-time social custom loved by all participants. Field corn or popcorn grown on the farm which the children may have picked themselves should be used. The popcorn may be popped and eaten along with homemade grape juice or cider which the children and youth have made. The popcorn may also be strung for Christmas tree decorations. Square dancing or folk dancing might be an added attraction in the fall or winter.

— *Butchering day,* an event probably more appropriate for older youth. The butchering of hogs and the old fashioned ways of making lard, bacon, hams, and sausage might be demonstrated.

— *Maple syrup production,* an exciting late winter or early spring event in those regions where hard (sugar) maples grow. The tapping of trees, collection of sap into buckets hung beneath spigots inserted into holes in the tree, the gathering of sap, and boiling it over a log fire in a sugarbush shack is a most pleasurable and educational experience. Children enjoy tasting the sap as it drips from the trees, and then tasting it again when it has been boiled into syrup. Further boiling will yield maple sugar which children can mold into candies. Pouring fresh syrup on clean snow makes maple "ice cream."

— *Quilting bees* usually appeal to older girls. Part of the fun is in collecting remnants and using patterns which grandma and great-grandma once used.

— *Candle making,* a popular activity at any time of year, but particularly around Christmas time. Authentic old candle molds and methods should be used.

— *Soap making,* an appropriate activity for a children's farm, because it was a necessary event on all old-time farms. Youngsters enjoy producing soap, because it is something they can take home and use.

— *Churning milk* for *butter making* in authentic churns, an exciting experience for youngsters who find it hard to believe that churning

[1] A Pennsylvania Dutch term for cutting apples in a particular way for making apple butter.

liquid milk will produce solid butter. For a treat, youngsters can eat the butter on rolls, biscuits, bread, or muffins which they themselves have baked.

— *Ice cream making,* probably *the* favorite farm-related activity of children and youth. The process of milking cows, using an antique ice cream freezer, following an old family recipe, to eating the delicious final product may be carried out in its entirety.

— *Dye making,* a fascinating activity. Many colors may be made from certain weeds, plants, and trees, including those which children have grown expressly for this purpose. Youngsters have fun and learn by experimenting with the preparation of dyes and the transformation of clothing, yarn, and curtains into a myriad of colors, using traditional methods.

— *Gathering honey* from beehives, an adventurous activity for most youngsters.

— *Pony* and *horse rides,* appealing to all children, from toddlers to sophisticated teenagers.

— *Sheep shearing,* enjoyable both for younger children who may only watch and for older youth who may actually do the shearing.

— *Lumberjack day* on the "back forty," a day-long event, beginning with a lumberman's breakfast cooked outdoors, land log rolling, sawing contests, and a tall tale telling contest.

— *Arbor day,* a time devoted to conservation practices, especially the planting of trees and shrubs at various locations on the farm for different purposes. Youngsters enjoy returning to the farm periodically during ensuing months to view the growth and development of trees or shrubs they planted.

— A *fish derby,* a fun-filled event for young people who love to fish. Held at the farm pond or stream, contests may be held for the most fish caught, largest fish landed, and other criteria.

— A *farm auction* with a youthful auctioneer, an activity new to many youngsters. An auction is as enjoyable to the young as to adults.

— *Hayrides* and *wagon rides* in the autumn on evenings when there is a "harvest moon" are often unforgettable events in the lives of youngsters. Such rides are usually followed by gathering around a bonfire, roasting weiners or marshmallows, and singing favorite songs.

— *Hunting* for *Indian artifacts,* a popular activity in the spring when farm fields are newly plowed and dragged.

— A *trading ring,* a special event which appeals to the barter spirit in humans. Youngsters bring to the ring whatever possessions they wish to trade and attempt to receive something more desirable.

— *Mushroom hunting,* an activity limited to approximately two weeks in the spring. With proper adult guidance, youngsters seek and pick the morel and other edible mushrooms. On a farm mushrooms are frequently found in or near the orchard, as well as in the woodlot.

— *Nut gathering* in autumn, a favorite pastime of children. Walnuts, butternuts, hickory, hazel, and other nuts are sought for food and crafts activities.

— *Berry picking* in domestic berry patches and those in the wild, fun for children who usually eat as much as they place in their baskets. Nothing is quite equal to the taste of the wild strawberry which graces most farm lands. Wild blackberries usually grow profusely on farms, and in some areas of the country wild blueberries may be found. In a few states domestic and wild cranberries may also be sought.

— *Harvesting wild rice.* This appeals to the older youth who must use special means for gathering this infrequently found crop.

— A winter moonlight *sleigh ride* with blankets, warm soapstones, and horses strung with bells, a memorable activity. A farm becomes a mystical place for children in such conditions.

— Old-fashioned *ice skating parties* on the farm pond accompanied by a bonfire, wiener roast, and music—further proof that the winter season on a farm can be an exciting time.

— *Barn dances.* Square, round, and folk dances provide color and gaiety to life on the farm at all times of the year.

— A *rural party-line telephone* system may be installed connecting various buildings on the farm. This was often a form of recreation in years past. Children will delight in "ringing up" friends in the barn, shed, or elsewhere, and in listening to others' conversations.

— An *antique show,* of interest to older children. The antiques may be brought by youngsters from their own homes, provided by local adults, or contributed by an antique dealer. They may be for display only, or offered for sale or trade. The antiques should be selected to represent the tradition and history of the area, particularly of the farm life in the region.

— Various demonstrations of *homemaking arts.* These activities should invite the participation of youngsters. They include weaving with a loom, baking bread, dyeing, canning, drying apples, constructing an egg tree at Easter time, making wreaths and other Christmas decorations, and braiding rugs.

— A *pumpkin carving* event, a favorite late October activity on the farm. Prizes may be given to the best work.

— *Crafts fairs* and *shows.* Held at various times of the year, these are popular gatherings at which youngsters and local craftsmen demonstrate their skills, and display and sell their products. Woodcarving, basket making, corn shuck art, lapidary, pottery, sandpainting, and other crafts are highlighted.

— *Historical and special pioneer celebrations* are appropriate and exciting occurrences on a children's farm. Children enjoy dressing up and re-enacting past dramatic times.

— An old-time *country fair.* This may be considered the highlight of all the special events on a children's farm. A fair may include a horse-pulling contest, livestock showing and judging, a greased

pig catching contest, country music, a sheep shearing contest, and showing and judging of homemaking activities including foods, clothing, and crafts.
— *Bobsledding* in the winter over snowy fields and country roads, an activity rarely equaled in providing fun and excitement to youngsters.

10

Children's Nature Areas

NATURE AREAS DESIGNED and developed for children and youth are popular places for play and learning. Some are provided by public park and recreation services, while others are part of agency programs and public school systems.

Value

Such areas supply youngsters with outdoor experiences which help to develop an awareness and appreciation of nature. Children learn to understand their relationship to other living things, and the role of humans in the ecological system.

These areas of natural beauty are rare commodities for many urban youngsters who are dissociated from nature. When children and youth are involved in the actual development and improvement of nature areas, they gain a satisfaction in knowing they have created and preserved beauty.

Outdoor experiences are often significant learning opportunities. Children learn skills, concepts, facts, generalizations, attitudes, and values.

Children and youth gain experiences which may influence their choice of future vocations.

Plants, aquatic life, animals, birds, and other living things are often saved from the destructive technology of man through the establishment of a nature area.

Types

Children's nature areas range in character from simple to complex, in size from an acre or less to thousands of acres, and in location from school sites to isolated rural state recreation areas. Most of these places have one main natural feature, such as a pond; others have several features, such as a stream, pine tree plantation, and a gravel pit.

Some children's nature areas began as a vacant lot. With careful planning and planting they have become rich nature resource areas. Other nature areas were unwanted swamps and trash dumps until someone realized their potential.

A most unusual children's nature area is a deep ravine approximately two and one-half city blocks long and one city block wide, adjacent to an elementary school and a junior high school. The ravine has a stream running through it, and youngsters have dug two shallow ponds for ducks and turtles. An open air amphitheater has been constructed, along with observation decks for astronomy and bird watching, and nature trails. A number of trees and a rose hedge have been planted. This simple nature area is used extensively by children, parents, and teachers.

Some nature areas are simply a small stand of hardwood trees. Others are a school forest planted in the late 1930s and 1940s. A nature center in one of our western states covers 2,000 acres of natural prairie land.

Many nature areas are principally bird sanctuaries. Others focus upon aquatic life. Trees, wildflowers, or a combination of the preceding are the main highlights of others.

Natural Features

The basic natural features of children's nature areas are trees and plants, water areas, wildlife, and various elevations. The most comprehensive nature areas will include the following: geological features, biological features, water resources, and historical and cultural features.

Specific natural components or features of children's nature areas are listed below:

— Lagoon
— Flowering shrubs
— Nut trees or grove
— Coniferous and deciduous trees
— Cactus
— Gravel pit
— Wildflowers
— Lake
— Stream
— Pond
— Swamp
— Low depressed area
— Bog
— Spring
— Waterfall
— Dead logs and log piles

— Brush piles
— Wildlife including animals, birds, reptiles, insects, fish, and other aquatic life
— Eroded soil area and soil profile
— Meadows
— Tree stumps
— Shrub and bush areas
— Bee tree
— Rock pile
— Demonstration plantings of wildlife food and cover-producing plants, shrubs, and trees
— "Keyed plantation"—the systematic planting of trees representative of a variety of types arranged according to leaf characteristics.
— Swales
— Ditches
— Fence rows
— Old orchards
— Wooden fences
— Hollow trees
— Standing dead trees
— Caves
— Rock outcroppings
— Ravines
— Indian mounds
— Cliffs
— Sand dunes

A typical nature area on a school site might include the following natural components: bulb beds, rock garden, watershed demonstration area, dwarf fruit trees, nature trail, tree nursery, rock retaining wall, fern garden, soil profile demonstration, swamp, observation hill, boulders, stream, pond and nesting island, tree and shrub windbreaks, burned over plot, ground cover plants, wildflowers, bee tree, woodlot, bittersweet arbor, grape arbor, plus the wildlife which normally inhabit such an area.

Facilities and Features

Physical facilities and features which further develop, complement, and interpret the natural features of children's nature areas are important to identify. The following may be provided:

— Weather station
— Animal shelters such as squirrel boxes
— Animal and bird feeding stations

— Bird baths
— Nature interpretation building for indoor activities during poor weather, for nature exhibits, including "Do Touch" displays, dioramas showing natural and pioneer history, taxidermy activities, and care of injured wildlife until sufficiently strong to return outdoors
— Observation piers, platforms, and rafts on ponds and lakes
— Log and stone resting and conversation benches
— Water bubbler to keep portion of pond or lake from icing over in winter so wild fowl and fish will be protected from "winter kill"
— Binocular or telescopic viewer for a high elevation lake, or swamp area
— Insect collecting station
— Rock retaining well at an eroding slope constructed of differing kinds of rock
— "Explorers' Headquarters," a replica of early American trading outposts. This may serve as the center for a variety of exploratory trips. Children may be outfitted as Davy Crocketts, prospectors, or trappers.
— Bird banding station
— Outdoor cooking and picnicking area
— "Pull it yourself" ferry for crossing a pond, lake, or stream
— Outdoor open air amphitheater
— Trailside shelters
— Observation tower
— Greenhouse
— Fish hatchery
— "Sky lift" for cliffs and steep hill and mountain areas
— "Monkey bridges" made of rope across ravines and streams
— Pulley rides down ravines and cliffs
— Foot bridges and single log bridges across streams
— Single rope swings
— Bee hives
— Sundial
— "Footprint patio" showing different animal and wild fowl tracks imprinted in concrete
— Nature library housed in a nature interpretation center or separate building
— Meditation chapel built of natural materials such as field stones, and located at an appropriate site
— Boat livery renting canoes, rowboats, sailboats, fishing tackle, and selling fish bait
— Bike livery renting bicycles
— Livery renting equipment for spelunking, rock and mountain climbing, and wood carving
— Ranges for field archery, miniature archery golf, target archery, clout shooting, and riflery where appropriate

An extensive nature area in the West is a unique combination of natural features and physical components. Spreading over 2,000 acres of native plains land, it is being restored to the condition it was in when the first homesteaders arrived in the area. Over 50 species of the original native plants grow there. Antelope, coyotes, badgers, skunks, horned toads, prairie dogs, jack and cotton-tailed rabbits, and other native animals populate the area. Over 40 species of birds may be seen. There are 7 miles of interpretive nature trails. Two authentic buffalo wallows, an erosion area, outdoor amphitheater, and sandstone fossils are featured.

The area's purposes are to achieve balance in nature, and to provide children and youth opportunities to experience the environment of pioneer days. An authentic two-room homestead sod house, completely furnished, has been built. A one-room sod school house with authentic furnishings has been constructed. Horse drawn farm machinery and equipment such as used by the early homesteaders, and an original covered wagon are unique and scarce artifacts of the center. Plans are to build a sod pioneer museum to house other household and agricultural antiques.

Nature Trails

The creation of trails throughout a children's nature area makes the resources and wonders of the area more accessible and intelligible to youngsters. It is recommended that trails be relocated from time to time to achieve different objectives and to prevent any portion of the area from becoming depleted from use. Youngsters should take part in the planning and fixing of trails.

Trails should connect varied outstanding or unique features of the nature area. They may have specific objectives or general exploration goals. They should be clearly marked so that youngsters need not be dependent upon trail leadership of others. Trails may be unmarked or marked by obvious signs such as piled stones, bent and tied twigs and grasses, keyed numbers, or wooden or metal plaques. The only marking a trail may require is a sign at its start stating, "Within the next 500 yards you may see. . . ." A waist-high rope will act as a trail guide for blind youngsters. Trails may be short or long, or be spur or closed "U" trails which lead back to the entrance area. Sometimes they are constructed to have unusual points of interest as their goal. Nature areas with extensive water areas, such as lagoons and connected lakes and ponds, can have unique and exciting canoe or rowboat nature trails, marked by floats or buoys. At some children's nature areas youngsters are provided with an "Explorer's Map" which outlines all of the trails and features of the area.

Trails vary markedly in type. The following are some of the common and uncommon ones:

- "Tasting Trail" or "Tastee Trail," where "Nature Detectives" taste sumac seeds, sassafras leaves, bark, or roots, mustard, rhubarb, watercress, leek, wild strawberries, wild blackberries, paw paws, green apples, wintergreen berries, and catnip, among other plants
- Canoe trip trail
- Bicycle trail, sometimes over an old railroad bed
- Cross-country ski trail
- Bluff edge trail
- Lake edge trail
- Fence row trail
- "Do Touch Trail" or "Tactile Trail"
- "Don't Touch Trail" to include poison ivy, water hemlock, sheep laurel, nettle, and similar plants
- "Medicine Man Trail" which includes medicinal herbs
- Compass trail to be explored with compass and map
- Pony trail, if appropriate
- "Scent Trail" including mints and odiferous plants and trees such as sassafras and balsam fir
- Sketching and photography trail
- Snow shoe trail
- Listening trail
- Blossom trail in the springtime
- Trails leading to bird and animal feeding stations
- Beauty trail
- Willow whistle trail leading to a willow tree grove to secure materials for the making of slip bark whistles
- Crafts materials trails leading to a gravel pit, clay bank, honeysuckle vines, or basswood tree
- Swamp trail
- Trail to fishing area
- Turtle pond trail
- Wildflower glen trail
- Lookout point trail
- Fire wood trail
- Wild foods trail
- Owl pellet trail
- Meditation-inspiration trail
- "Forest Inns Trail" leading to hollow trees inhabited by birds and animals
- Raccoon Hollow trail
- Eagles' Nest trail
- Campfire ring trail

The preceding trails suggest kinds of hikes which can be made. It is also possible to have a nighttime hike, beeline hike, bird, animal, tree, and plant identification hikes, butterfly hike, winter exploration hike, or color hike.

Special Stations

Learning stations are usually established or identified within a children's nature area. These are considered highlights and may include spots where plants thrive or animals nest, including a raccoon's den, great blue heron nesting area on the edge of a lake or marsh, an eagle's nest, beaver dam, waterfall, cave, and a swimming hole with a diving tree and a rope swing tied to a tree limb overhanging the water. Children and youth usually want to spend a lot of time at such stations.

Planning and Development

No children's nature area will ever be found in perfect condition and containing optimum resources. Careful planning should take place to insure the maximum usage of available resources. While adult leadership and involvement will always be necessary, youngsters benefit by taking an active role in the development of a nature area. They may gain from this experience an ecological outlook that combines awareness and appreciation of the outdoors with action appropriate to their age and experience.

Developmental activities include land reforestation with coniferous and deciduous trees, stream bank improvement, pruning and thinning of plants and trees, trail building, planting of food-producing shrubs and bushes for wildlife, pond digging or cleaning, building brush piles, establishing living snow and wind buffers, building retaining walls, spreading shredded bark or wood on trails, transplanting wildflowers which have been salvaged from the paths of road builders and other construction machines, and carrying out periodic surveys of plant, tree, animal, bird, insect, and aquatic life to determine what progress is being made and what yet needs to be done.

Special Events

Many special events may take place. They are often too complex or involved to occur more frequently than weekly, monthly, or seasonally. Here are a few:

— An *annual bird census* is usually carried out in a nature area during the winter or in early spring before leaves appear on the trees. At this time youngsters try to identify and record as many different species of birds as possible.
— *Arbor Day* or *Earth Day* occurs in the springtime. Children and

youth plant trees, engage in other conservation practices, and sometimes release pheasant chicks and fish fingerlings on the site.

— *Bird banding* is a special activity which requires licensed adult leadership.

— *Live animal trapping* is an interesting process involving setting up and caring for trapping lines to capture animals for census purposes.

— *Outdoor skills contests* include archery shoots and canoe competition (racing, jousting, and bobbing).

— *Color tours* of the nature area in autumn are carried out by rowboat, canoe, or on foot.

— *Outdoor photography* exhibits and contests are interesting.

— *Celebrations of natural events* such as the Buzzard Festival of an Ohio community (when the buzzards return to the area on a certain day each year after wintering in the South), or celebrations of Indian lore and historical occurrences are indeed special.

— *Fishing derbies* are contests at which prizes are awarded.

Other special events are possible: *night campfires, astronomy study evenings,* or *outdoor musical concerts.*

Outdoor survival workshops can help youngsters learn how to live off the land and construct survival shelters.

Correlated Activities

Children and youth enjoy participating in activities related to the main experiences offered in nature areas. Several of these are outlined below:

— *Publication of a "Nature Newspaper"* which might be named "Rocks and Rills," "Trails and Tales," or "Birds and Bogs" could be written by the youngsters themselves with the purpose of sharing ideas, happenings, information, feelings, and concerns about the outdoors and their nature area.

— *Nature crafts* using the natural materials found right in the area might include wood carving, lapidary activities, clay preparation, sculpture, and firing, making natural dyes and coloring cloth, nature rubbings, construction of nature mobiles and collages, sand painting, sand casting, weaving with cattail leaves, basketry, Indian basswood cordage, making musical instruments, fashioning archery bows, and constructing bird and animal houses and feeding stations.

— *Wild food* identification, collection, and preparation is a fascinating activity to many youngsters.

— *Nature collections* including leaves, fossils, Indian arrowheads and other artifacts, shells, owl pellets (and their dissection) are interesting experiences.

1

How to Plan, Develop, and Operate Creative Outdoor Play Areas

PLANNING, BUILDING, AND OPERATING creative outdoor play areas should involve a number of activities, particularly if the play areas are on school sites, inner-city land, or large public parks. Obviously, private home play areas do not require the extensive planning, development, and operation procedures that other play areas demand.

Planning and Development

Thorough planning prior to, and during, the operation of a creative outdoor play area is vital to its acceptance, use, and success. Planning should involve all those, at least on a representative basis, who will eventually be participants in, or affected by, the creative outdoor play area. This means that youngsters as well as adults representing various interests should take part in planning and development; they should be meaningfully involved.

An advisory or planning and development committee with the following membership, and with the actual power to make decisions and guide the development of the play area, is most effective. This committee should be formed of interested persons; in addition, some thought might be given to securing three special kinds of people: (1) "arrangers" or well-known people who will be able to open doors and secure resources by reason of their prestige or importance; (2) "planners" who will have vision and creativity to project what *might* be; and (3) "doers" who will actually carry out the ideas and plans of the committee and make visible progress.

The committee must accomplish some specific steps which are critical in the planning and development process:

1. Identify or view the play-learning needs and interests of children and youth. If the play area is to be for one particular age group, then the focus should be upon the needs and interests of that group. Play area planning must be built upon real needs and interests.
2. Visit and study existing outdoor play areas in the community, if there are any, and collect data identifying their strengths and weaknesses.

3. Ascertain the degree to which the play and learning needs and interests of youngsters are being met. Collect baseline data on their present status. Identify specific areas of weakness and strength, and changes to be sought.
4. Make visits to outdoor play areas in operation in other locales to learn about their problems.
5. Survey existing community resources:
   a) *People* with skills, knowledge, or interest in creative outdoor play areas—educators, parents, youth, businessmen, and others.
   b) Possible new *sites* for developing play areas.
   c) *Equipment, materials,* and *tools.*
   d) Books, periodicals, articles, slides, films, and other *audiovisual resources* to provide ideas.
   e) Possible sources of *funding* or *donations* in terms of money, equipment and supplies, land, and people's time.

   All identified resources, even the names of individual persons and their skills or potential donations, might be listed and described on cards and then filed for future reference and use.
6. Share the committee's purpose and progress to date with "power people," those in formal and informal positions of leadership (including opinion leaders) in the community. They must be persuaded of the worth of the endeavor, and asked to legitimize or sanction it. They might be included in the planning and development process either as members of the committee or in some less formal way. If this is not accomplished, the endeavor may be undermined by these "power people" at a later time.
7. Select a site, if necessary.
8. Devise specific plans for building or rebuilding the creative outdoor play area. Sketch them out on paper, and make measurements on the site. Plans should conform to the needs and interests of children and youth which were earlier identified.
9. Identify priorities for implementing the plans. Answer questions such as: Which areas and pieces of equipment will be most useful to the youngsters during the present and the coming seasons of the year? Which are simple enough so that they can be implemented without delay? A timetable for step-by-step implementation of the plans, or a "PERTing" chart, should be set up.

   In situations where several creative outdoor play areas are being developed, such as when all the elementary school playgrounds in a community are undergoing plans for change, another important step in the planning process is desirable: Before new plans are implemented on a full scale, it would be wise to carry out first a "trial plot," or pilot project, on one or two play areas for an adequate length of time. Agriculture, business, and industry almost always try out new ideas on a limited basis before expanding them to full operation. A pilot project involving one or two school playgrounds, a small city park, or one roadside park,

for a period of several months or a year, would be a wise procedure. This would afford adequate time to evaluate results, test economic feasibility, work out unexpected problems, and widely publicize the project. If the pilot project should prove unsuccessful, it would be easier to terminate plans at this time before widespread implementation of the master plan, or correct problems, change emphases and procedures, or continue the pilot project with modifications for another trial period.
10. Share plans, priorities, and timetable with "power people" and maintain or gain their support.

Implementation of Plans

The implementation of plans for a creative outdoor play area includes several major steps:

1. Secure the new site or obtain formal permission to rebuild the old, whatever the case may be.
2. Obtain commitments from "workers," whether they be youth, volunteer adults, or others for carrying out specific jobs.
3. Gather equipment, materials contributions, and tools.
4. Organize task forces and leaders for the various kinds of work to be done, including alteration of terrain, planting, and equipment construction; then devise a work schedule.
5. Supervise the work of the task forces.
6. Keep "power people" and others informed of progress.

Evaluation

Evaluation should be an important and integral part of the entire process of planning, developing, implementing, and operating creative outdoor play areas. It is needed in order to ascertain the type of learning occurring in children, to identify weaknesses and strengths of the play area, and to make decisions regarding its continuing operation. Several elements of evaluation should be given attention.

Baseline evaluation. Baseline data sl ould be collected as the initial step in the development of a creative outdoor play area. Conditions existing before the operation of the "new" play area should be described and documented. Unless this is accomplished, it will be impossible at a later date to describe the changes in children, and factors affected by the "new" play area.

Related to the collecting of baseline data might be the wish of some evaluators to carry out longitudinal studies of children and others who utilize the creative outdoor play area. These studies may begin with the gathering of baseline data, then continue with the regular collection of certain data over a period of 5, 10, or even 25 years. Few studies of long-range outcomes are ever carried out. Such studies can be very helpful in providing information about children's growth and development patterns, individual leisure-time activities, and family life.

Product evaluation.   Product evaluation should be carried out periodically. "Product," as used here, refers to the measurable changes occurring in children through play in the cognitive, psychomotor or affective areas; for the most part products are short-term results. Products may be identified in terms of certain movement patterns or skills to be achieved, a certain level of leg strength to be reached, concepts or facts to be acquired, or attitudes towards self or others to be developed. The goals and objectives guiding the products sought may vary from one creative outdoor play area to another. For example, the major goals and objectives of a play area on an elementary school site may relate only to the acquisition of basic movement patterns, agility, balance, and physical fitness in the youngsters who use that play area. On the other hand, the major goals and objectives of a play area on a small space in an inner city area may relate primarily to the growth and improvement of social relations among youngsters of diverse racial backgrounds.

Process evaluation.   The process of program development and operation should be evaluated. This assessment should focus on the following concerns: the extent to which parents are aware of the objectives and goals of the particular play area; the degree to which key people or "power people" have been kept informed of activities; how well community resources are identified and utilized; the extent to which youngsters are involved in guiding the development and operation of the area; the effectiveness of the planning committee in carrying out their timetable of events.

Evaluation methods and instruments.   Numerous kinds of evaluation techniques and instruments should be identified in order to collect data and analyze the degree and quality of change. Both obtrusive and unobtrusive data may be collected and used. Evaluation methods and instruments can include: parental observations; child interviews and surveys; unsolicited testimony or reaction by youngsters; degree of visible wear of equipment, surfaces, and topographical features; number of children and youth using the area at various times of the day, season, and year; amount of use by various age groups; number and kinds of accidents reported; degree of vandalism; unsolicited teacher or other adult testimony; case histories of individual youngsters; number of discipline problems; amount of publicity in the mass media; degree of individual versus group activity; amount of PTA, community service club, and other community participation and support; formal evaluation by a team of experts from another community; informal adult observations; evaluations of children's fitness, motor skill, social position, self-esteem, visual perception, and language development; written interest and attitude surveys; and 8mm motion picture films and analyses.

Informal evaluation. Evaluation may also be conducted in informal ways. Simple observation of youngsters using a creative outdoor play area over a short or long period of time will provide a lot of data. Questions such as the following might be asked and answered: Does the area allow for group play activities? Are there opportunities for children to play alone? Do the participants seem to be enjoying themselves? What age groups are using what kinds of equipment and terrain? Are there pieces of equipment not being utilized? Is there evidence of creative expression through play? Do youngsters spend time waiting in line for turns to use certain pieces of equipment? Is the area aesthetically pleasing?

Continuing and Expanding Operation

A continuing advisory committee composed of representatives of all involved and interested groups should be established to carry out further planning and provide guidance and leadership in the current operation of the play area. Changes based upon the results of continuing evaluation should be effected. Resources in the community must be continually identified and solicited. Repairs and other types of refurbishing activities must be carried out. Needs and interests of youngsters must be assessed periodically so that the play area remains a place designed truly for them.

12

Special
Events

A NUMBER OF SPECIAL EVENTS may be held at the creative outdoor play area throughout the year. Some would be seasonal occasions; others could be planned for any time. Most of those proposed below require some adult or older youth leadership. Such supervision might be provided by teachers, parents, paraprofessionals, playground supervisors, high school students, college students, or senior citizens.

Some Suggestions

The following are only a few possibilities. Many of these ideas will suggest to the reader other special events. In addition, youngsters themselves will think up many possibilities for special occasions.

Paint-in. This event would involve youngsters in a variety of art activities, including the group activity of painting a mural on a concrete, brick, or wooden wall as a somewhat permanent "work of art"; doing paintings or drawings on butcher paper or brown paper; and making nature "rubbings" from the surfaces of rocks and boulders, tree bark, and other natural objects. The finished products could be displayed for all to see on a wall, hung from a piece of equipment, or exhibited in an indoor spot.

Sculpture fair. Group or individual sculpturing of wet sand, snow, ice blocks, or mud would be the purpose of this event. Prizes could be given, and accomplishments displayed.

Challenge course contest. As individuals, or members of teams, youngsters would compete against time as they perform the varied skills required in a predetermined "challenge course" (obstacle course). Two or three different courses might be set up, appropriate to the various age groups which would be participating. Obviously, what would be appropriate and challenging for upper elementary school children would be different from that suitable for preschoolers.

Nature Games. Orienteering [1] and other compass games, nature scavenger hunts, nature identification games, and rope tying could be taught and played.

Field day. This event could be provided for all age groups. Youngsters would compete as individuals, or as individuals representing designated teams. There would be individual and team contests, such as land log-rolling, high jumping, running races, stilt walking contests, relays, distance ball throws, climbing events, all utilizing much of the equipment to be found in the play area.

Work-in. This would be a day during which the area would be cleaned up, equipment painted, new equipment constructed, and trees and shrubs planted. Such a day would be especially appropriate at a time when there is much national concern about the quality of the outdoor environment.

Old-time games day. This would be a day set aside for the learning and playing of the old favorite games which many of today's children and youth have never played. Such games as hoop rolling, kick the can, prisoner goal, pom-pom pull away, and variations of marbles would be introduced. Many adults would enjoy participating in the planning and operation of this event (see Appendix).

Carnival. Booths made and operated by youngsters would provide all the members of the community, young and old, with opportunities to try their luck and skill at various kinds of contests. For a penny or two, or a token booth fee (the proceeds could go towards the purchase of something needed for the play area, or could cover some of the supplies needed for the carnival), individuals could participate in bean bag throwing, "tightrope" walking, basket shooting, or dart throwing at balloons. An old-time popcorn wagon could be secured to provide the flavor of yesteryear's carnivals—as well as something to eat.

Dramatics and talent show. The talents of young and old community members in puppet shows, plays, and performances would be offered throughout a day and evening. The various shows could be scheduled ahead of time for viewing at particular times during the day. A booth could teach make-up techniques to aspiring actors and actresses. Everyone attending this event could be required to dress up in costumes in order to gain admittance to the festivity. A play area with an outdoor amphitheater, such as mentioned earlier in this book, would be an ideal spot for the various activities of this day.

[1] A complex compass and cross-country hiking activity.

Bicycle—tricycle parade.   Youngsters would be encouraged to decorate their bikes or tricycles for this event. A parade through the play area could be held, and prizes given for the best decorations. Various bicycle and tricycle riding contests could be held; events such as riding around flags, riding on a chalk line, and trick riding, could be awarded prizes.

Camping caravan or holiday.   At this event children, youth, and adults would be taught different camping skills, including fire-building techniques, outdoor cooking, pitching tents, constructing lean-tos, and lashing. Those who own tents could be encouraged to bring and set them up; local sporting goods merchants might be invited to display tents and other outdoor camping aids.

Ice skating carnival.   This could be an evening event for youngsters or adults or families. Features of old-time skating parties, such as music, a bonfire, marshmallow roast, and races, could be included.

Plant-in.   This occasion would be centered around the cultivation of some out-of-the-way piece of land within the play area, and planting bulbs, such as crocuses, tulips, hyacinths, and daffodils, which would bloom the following spring. Most children are intrigued by the process of planting and growing. Such an event would also contribute to the beauty of the area.

Archery golf tournament.   If the play area has enough space, an archery golf course could be laid out for a tourney which could last a day or two. This sport is a relatively new one, and exciting to both youngsters and adults.

Plug golf tournament.   Using painted plywood discs laid on the ground as targets, competition in casting skills, as used in fishing, could be offered to youth or adults. It is not necessary to have access to water to implement this kind of tournament.

Cement autographing or cement sign-in.   This event would provide an opportunity which many children long to have. If a portion of the play area is to be poured with cement for a new surface, youngsters could be invited to make a hand print, footprint, or scratch their initials in the wet cement. Months and years later, the same youngsters would be able to see their initials, or measure the growth of their hands and feet.

Kite making and flying day.   Newspapers, butcher paper, or brown paper could be supplied to or brought by youngsters to make kites. A number of different kite designs could be taught and tried. Youngsters could decorate their kites according to their own imaginations. Contests could be held for kite design, and for flying.

Sidewalk art day. On a particular day, every interested child and youth could be allotted one square of concrete sidewalk, or a space on an asphalt or concrete surface to decorate as they please with colored chalk. There would be judging and prizes awarded for various categories.

Pet parade and contest. Pets of every kind would be brought to the play area in appropriate containers or on leashes. They could be paraded across the area by their proud owners, and then judged for beauty, homeliness, and size, among other categories.

Appendix

Values of Creative Outdoor Play Areas Summarized

THE VALUES OF CREATIVE outdoor play areas are many. They accrue to preschool, elementary, and secondary school children and youth, as well as teachers, school administrators, parents and families, governmental agency officials, and other community people who become involved, directly or indirectly, in the development of creative outdoor play areas. The following are the most significant values of these programs:

1. Opportunities are provided for creative expression by participants.
2. Motor growth and development, including perceptual-motor skills and physical fitness, are promoted.
3. Social growth and development are promoted.
4. Mental growth and development are promoted.
5. Emotional growth and development are promoted.
6. Opportunities are provided for youngsters to learn about, live in, and experience a wholesome outdoor environment where they may escape temporarily from the closeness of small urban spaces and playing in the streets.
7. Ample opportunities for self-directed and self-devised experiences for exploring and learning are provided to youngsters.
8. Children and youth are given a new understanding of themselves and their peers, as they play together in another type of learning environment. Through play, children and youth of different racial, socio-economic, physical, emotional, and intellectual backgrounds learn to know and understand each other.
9. Youngsters are afforded experiences which help them build their individual value systems.
10. Children and youth are introduced to skills and interests which will lead to constructive use of free time in the present and in future adult years.
11. Opportunities are afforded for the development of leadership qualities in youngsters who are not usually leaders at school, at play, or at home; they can start "fresh" here.
12. Teachers, recreation leaders, and parents are enlightened by new perceptions of individual needs, strengths, and interests, because the adults can see the youngsters in new roles in a new setting.

13. Children and youth are provided opportunities for outdoor play in all seasons.
14. Opportunities are made available for family visits and participation.
15. Opportunities are created for the enhancement of and integration with the regular school curriculum.
16. Planning, development, and operation processes may be seen as providing abundant opportunities for meaningful volunteer participation by community businessmen, retired adults, nonworking mothers, and other community laymen. Such community involvement in projects for youngsters increases community unity, and provides opportunities for adults and youth to better understand each other.
17. Opportunities for meaningful work experiences are opened to upper elementary and secondary school youth.
18. The beautification and "greening" of inner city lots, city playgrounds, school sites, backyards, and other areas is accomplished. The attractiveness of a neighborhood and the general appearance of an entire community or city are enhanced.

Old Time Outdoor Games

Many of today's youngsters have missed playing old-time outdoor games. These games were a real part of the childhood culture of the past. Perhaps they are not known and played to any great extent now because of the lack of space in which to run (most of the games are characterized by running), the changed ideas of leisure of today's children and young people, and the failure of many parents to spend time teaching their children games and skills.

Whatever the reason, these almost forgotten outdoor games contribute much to youngsters' learning in the psychomotor, cognitive, and affective domains. They also are good sources of pure excitement and enjoyment. This generation of children should not be deprived of the happiness which other generations of children experienced through playing the older outdoor games.

The following games and activities are but a few of many. The reader will undoubtedly be reminded of others to add to the list. Notice that most of the games use the natural large muscle movement patterns of youngsters, especially running.

For all seasons:

— Setting the Pegs
— Run Sheep Run
— Prison Goal
— Red Light, Green Light
— Three Old Cats

— Pom Pom Pull Away
— Capture the Flag
— Hide and Seek
— Kick the Can
— Variations of Tag
— Bandana Parachutes

Seasonal:

— Fox and Geese
— Kite Flying
— Snowshoeing
— Snow Sculpturing
— Variations of Hockey
— Variations of Marbles

Descriptions and rules of these games, if not known to the reader, may be found in old game books and some newer comprehensive ones. An adult, especially a senior citizen, would probably be able to tell how these games are played, and offer additional ideas.

Selected References

Articles

Grey, Alexander, "Creative Learning in Children's Playgrounds," *Childhood Education,* May, 1969, pp. 491–99.

Hanson, Robert F., "Playgrounds Designed for Adventure," *Journal of Health, Physical Education and Recreation (JOHPER),* May, 1969, pp. 34–36.

"Great Places to Play," *House and Garden,* May, 1969, pp. 116–17.

Smith, Julian W., "Outdoor Education for Lifetime Interests," *Childhood Education,* October, 1967, pp. 79–81.

Books and booklets

Children's Rooms and Play Yards. Menlo Park, California: Lane Magazine and Book Company (Lane Books), 1960 and 1970 (2nd ed.).

Friedberg, M. Paul, *Playgrounds for City Children.* Washington, D.C.: Association for Childhood Education International, 1969.

Ledermann, Alfred, and Alfred Trachsel, *Creative Playgrounds and Recreation Centers* (rev. ed.). New York/Washington, D.C.: Frederick A. Praeger, Inc., 1968.

Miller, Peggy L., *Outdoor Creative Play Areas.* East Lansing, Mich.:

Outdoor Education Project and Council on Outdoor Education and Camping of the A.A.H.P.E.R., 1969.

――――, *School Gardens and Farms—Aspects of Outdoor Education.* Las Cruces, New Mexico: Educational Resources Information Center (ERIC), Clearinghouse on Rural Education and Small Schools (CRESS), December, 1970.

Nash, Jay B., *Philosophy of Recreation and Leisure.* Dubuque, Iowa: William C Brown Co., Publishers, 1953.

See, Frederic C., *Grand Rapids Park Story.* Grand Rapids, Mich.: Park Department, City of Grand Rapids, n.d.

Smith, Julian W., Reynold E. Carlson, George W. Donaldson, and Hugh B. Masters, *Outdoor Education.* Englewood Cliffs, N.J.: Prentice-Hall, Inc., 1963 and 1972 (rev. ed.).

Williams, Wayne R., *Recreation Places.* New York: Reinhold Publishing Corp., 1958.

Index